Blended Learning

Using technology in and beyond the language classroom

Pete Sharma & Barney Barrett

MACMILLAN

Macmillan Education
Between Towns Road, Oxford OX4 3PP
A division of Macmillan Publishers Limited
Companies and representatives throughout the world

ISBN 978-0-230-02083-2

First published 2007

Note to Teachers

Designed by Anthony Godber
Cover design by Andrew Oliver
Cover photograph by Corbis/Simon Thorpe

Authors' acknowledgements

With thanks to Adrian Underhill for kicking
everything off and his encouragement along the way.
To Jill Florent for her early shaping of the work. To
Anna Cowper for her inspirational guidance and faith.
For their comments on an early draft which changed
the course of this book, Jim Scrivener and Michael
Carrier. To our Editor Nick Canham for his sensitive,
thoughtful input which helped to create the final
version. To Catriona Watson-Brown for all her work
on the text.

Thanks also to Michael Rundell and Katalin Sule
for their invaluable input on electronic dictionaries.
Hilary Nesi, Warwick University, for her input on
Portable Electronic Dictionaries. Anna Calvi for her
input and ideas on concordancing. Fiona MacKenzie,
Stuart Cochrane and colleagues at the Macmillan
English Campus. Christiane Khatchadourian and
Reinaldo Campos, Cultura Inglesa, São Paulo, Brasil,
for the practical idea 'Exploit the headline news'.
Tilly Harrison, Warwick University, for her input and
comments on wikis. Sophie Ioannou-Georgiou for
her smiles and input on Chat and the practical activity
'A weekend with a friend from out-of-town'. Kevin
Westbrook for his input on VLEs and the practical
idea 'Writing a business letter.' Sheila Vine and
Valentina Dodge for their input, ideas on 'blended
books' and the case study 'VLE'. Edward Bressan,
Oxford Brookes University, for his thoughts on
using VLEs. Francis Jones for his invaluable input
on interactive whiteboards and his practical ideas.
Cathy Yates for sharing her experiences on IWBs
and Barbara Buxton, Warwickshire College. Paul
East, Pyramid Consulting. Karen Richardson. To
Steve Lowe and all the teaching staff at Linguarama
Stratford for their continued interest in using
technology in their teaching and their willingness
to try out new things and ideas in the classroom. In
particular, to Joy Godwin for her enthusiasm for
digital audio recorders.

The publishers would like to thank Michael Carrier
and Jim Scrivener for their invaluable help and
practical advice on developing the manuscript.

The authors and publishers would like to thank
the following for permission to reproduce their
photographic material:
Audacity: Courtesy of Audacity http://audacity.
sourceforge.net/ p.118; British Broadcasting
Corporation: p.40; Cambridge University Press:
p.53(b), p.55(b), p.83; Google: © Google Inc and
used with permission p.30, p.115, p.116; Horizon
Wimba: © Horizon Wimba p.101; Microsoft:
Microsoft, p.71, p.80, p.85, p.87, p.88, p.102,
p.146; OneStopEnglish: p.37; Oxford Brookes
University: p.104(b),. p.105, p.107; Oxford
University Press, www.oup.com/elt/naturalenglish:
p.42; Pearson Education: p.57; Helene Rogers: p.95.

Printed and bound in Great Britain by Scotprint

2011 2010 2009 2008 2007

10 9 8 7 6 5 4 3 2 1

CONTENTS

ABOUT THE AUTHORS

Pete Sharma

Pete started his EFL career as a Business English teacher in Madrid, moving to Finland before returning to the UK. Variety is the spice of life, and the quest for variety has driven his work as a teacher, teacher trainer, Director of Studies and school manager. He became the training and development manager for Linguarama, a Business English organisation, and has inspected schools, taught writing seminars in the Middle and Far East, and helped create trainer training courses. Changing from ESP to EAP, he currently divides his time between lecturing at universities and writing. He is a self-confessed conference addict, presenting regularly at IATEFL and BESIG. The use of technology in language teaching really 'lights his fire', although spending six years to complete a Masters in Educational Technology and ELT may be stretching the point. He enjoys contributing to the profession through his blog, shared with co-author Barney. Now he has finished his dissertation, he can rediscover his family and devote time to tracking down rare Nick Cave albums.

Barney Barrett

Barney has worked as a Business English teacher for over 12 years. After a brief stint working in-company in Spain, he returned to the UK and settled down to work for Linguarama at their centre in Stratford-upon-Avon. It was here that he met Pete, and they quickly discovered a mutual interest in things computer-based. This resulted in their book *The Internet and Business English* (Summertown, 2003), which was Highly Commended in the Duke of Edinburgh English Speaking Union awards, occasional appearances at conferences and regular writing, such as their technology column in the BESIG newsletter. He is always on the look-out for ways to exploit new technologies and is sometimes to be seen not bent over a laptop computer updating and improving their website http://www.te4be.com.

Authors' note

While all the web addresses were correct and 'live' at the time of editing, the authors and publishers can accept no responsibility for URLs that change in the interim. Regular updates to this book can be found at the accompanying website (http://www.blendedlearning.com).

Dedication

Pete: to María and Jade for their love, support and patience.
Barney: to John and Mary Barrett for their love, moral and medical support.

ABOUT THE SERIES

Welcome to *Macmillan Books for Teachers.* Our titles are written by acknowledged and innovative leaders in each field to help you develop your teaching repertoire, practical skill and theoretical knowledge.

Suited to newer and experienced teachers, the series combines the best of classic teaching methodology with recent cutting-edge developments. Insights from academic research are combined with hands-on experience to create books which focus on real-world teaching solutions.

We hope you will find the ideas in them a source of inspiration in your own teaching and enjoyment in your professional learning.

Adrian Underhill

Titles in the series

An A–Z of ELT	Scott Thornbury
Beyond the Sentence	Scott Thornbury
Blended Learning	Barney Barrett and Pete Sharma
Children Learning English	Jayne Moon
Discover English	Rod Bolitho and Brian Tomlinson
Learning Teaching	Jim Scrivener
Sound Foundations	Adrian Underhill
Teaching Practice	Roger Gower, Diane Phillips and Steve Walters
Teaching Reading Skills	Christine Nuttall
Uncovering Grammar	Scott Thornbury
500 Activities for the Primary Classroom	Carol Read
700 Classroom Activities	David Seymour and Maria Popova

INTRODUCTION

For a long time now, we have been enthusiastic about using technology in language teaching, not only to support our efforts as teachers, but also to help students learn independently, outside the classroom. When we attend ELT conferences, we often here comments such as 'What's a wiki?' and 'How do you use a podcast?' One teacher complained, 'I wish the presenters wouldn't go around assuming we know what these things are.' It strikes us that those people who share our passion are already incorporating technology in their courses. However, many other teachers would like to use it more, but for a wide variety of reasons, they do not. Teachers may lack knowledge about technology or feel under-confident using a particular technology with their students. They may want more training; they may not have enough time to get familiar with the technology; or simply, they feel lacking in confidence because they fear that the technology will crash. This book has been written especially with these teachers in mind.

Before exploring this book, we recommend considering how much you know about technology in language teaching. It may be that you are a relative beginner to this area. Perhaps you know a lot about a particular technology (email or Internet) and very little about others (blogs or interactive whiteboards). You may know a lot about the actual technology itself, but very little about the applications of technology to ELT. You may already be very knowledgeable and be looking for new practical ideas. Whatever your particular situation, we urge you to use this book selectively. One approach would be to identify the gaps in your knowledge and go straight to those sections.

The main chapters in this book are laid out in such a way as to offer an introduction to each technology – with a description of what it is and how to use it. This is for those unfamiliar with a particular technology. Then, we describe the opportunities offered by using this technology, and flag up any issues. Each chapter concludes with a *Practical activities* section, which are designed to be easy to use, and sometimes a *Case studies* section, which provide information on real situations faced by teachers incorporating technology into their teaching.

Technology changes fast. This is why this book is supported by a website, created by our publishers, Macmillan. Here you will find regular announcements which update the contents of this book, as well as useful links and further ideas.

We hope you find this book useful and interesting; we hope it will change your teaching.

Barney Barrett and Pete Sharma

March 2007

BLENDED LEARNING: AN INTRODUCTION

This chapter will define and explore the term *blended learning*. It will look at the reasons why it is important for language teachers to incorporate technology into their courses, and focus on some factors influencing the uptake of technology.

What is blended learning?

Blended learning refers to a language course which combines a face-to-face (F2F) classroom component with an appropriate use of technology. The term *technology* covers a wide range of recent technologies, such as the Internet, CD-ROMs and interactive whiteboards. It also includes the use of computers as a means of communication, such as chat and email, and a number of environments which enable teachers to enrich their courses, such as VLEs (virtual learning environments) (see page 108), blogs (see page 115) and wikis (see page 119).

We will assume that you have decided to incorporate technology into a language course for a pedagogical reason, and by doing so, you are adding value to the teaching. We cover the use of technology inside the language classroom, as well as in support of a course where learners access technology between their classes. The book covers the use of technology in both structured ways, where learners work on specific tasks assigned by their teacher, and unstructured ways, where they browse materials and gain extra exposure and practice in the language.

A blended-learning course is potentially greater than the sum of its parts, and positive learning outcomes are most apparent when clear roles are assigned to the teacher and to the technology.

The term *blended learning* has been used for a long time in the business world. There, it refers to a situation where an employee can continue working full time and simultaneously take a training course. Such a training course may use a web-based platform. Many companies are attracted by the potential of blended learning as a way of saving costs; employees do not need to take time out of work to attend a seminar; they can work on their course in their own time, at their own convenience and at their own pace. Companies around the world have moved parts of their in-house training onto e-learning platforms, and use sophisticated tools such as learning-management systems in order to organize the course content. The mode of delivery may include CD-ROM, web-based training modules and paper-based manuals.

Many of the benefits described above are also applicable to language teaching. The term *blended learning* can be applied to a very broad range of teaching and learning situations. It is commonly applied to a course where all the learners meet with the teacher in a face-to-face (F2F) class, but in which the course includes a parallel self-study component such as a CD-ROM or access to web-based materials. Use of these elements may be optional. Learners can be set pre-lesson tasks or specific homework tasks between the F2F classes. It is becoming more frequent that the technology is always available in class, and is used as and when it is appropriate.

The term *blended learning* has a range of meanings. This is not a new phenomenon in ELT, where many terms have several interpretations – *task* and *authentic* for instance.

Here are a number of typical definitions:

- a 'combination of online and in-person, classroom learning activities'
  (http://www.cybermediacreations.com/elearning/glossary.htm)
- learning or training events or activities where e-learning, in its various forms, is combined with more traditional forms of training such as 'classroom' training
  (http://www.intelera.com/glossary.htm)
- the combination of multiple approaches to teaching or to educational processes which involve the deployment of a diversity of methods and resources
  (http://en.wikipedia.org/wiki/Blended_learning)
- combining … (different) web-based technologies
  (Driscoll)
- combining pedagogical approaches
  (Driscoll)
- a 'mixture of face-to-face … and distance learning'
  (Frendo, 2005)
- combining e-learning with … F2F
  (Smith and Baber, 2005)

For many, blended learning is 'nothing new' (Claypole, 2003) – merely the logical extension of what we do already. The term has also been criticized. It can be seen as a 'compromise' position. A blended-learning course run without a principled approach may be seen as an 'eclectic' blending together of course components, and can end up as rather a mish-mash. There may be little or no relation between the taught and the online components of a course. In a worst-case scenario, learners may suffer the 'worst of both worlds' – those not enjoying the online component being forced to participate in web-based communication, and those happier communicating online having to attend classes. On the other hand, done well, blended learning can exploit the best of both worlds. Carefully chosen online materials can enhance the classroom component of the course, and learners have the opportunity to work at their own pace and follow their own interests. The outside world can be brought into the classroom, improving motivation and generating interest. This chapter concludes with our own principles, which we feel important to delivering a blended-learning course.

An overview of this book

This book covers many of the growing range of technologies used in ELT, and describes how they can be integrated into a number of teaching and learning situations. The growth of the Internet has radically changed English-language teaching. Chapter 2 focuses on the Web, the part of the Internet where websites live. The chapter is divided into three sections: the first focuses on searching skills, and explores ways of searching more effectively; the second discusses ways of using some of the vast amount of authentic material available on the Web as part of a blended-learning language course; and the final section provides some practical ideas which you can incorporate into your teaching.

Chapter 3 looks at ELT material. It considers the way that the coursebook has been transformed and is now supported by a whole range of supplementary materials, including CD-ROM and online material on the publisher's website. The chapter also focuses on the Macmillan English Campus, which places a significant volume of learners' course material onto the Web for access within and outside the classroom. Finally, the chapter looks at some authoring tools which allow teachers to create interactive online materials for their own learners.

Chapter 4 looks at the opportunities afforded by electronic dictionaries. You may previously have raised learners' awareness of the benefits of using paper-based dictionaries. Today, learners have access to CD-ROM dictionaries and a range of dictionaries on the Web. They may bring electronic translators to the classroom. These tools help learners to develop their study skills and provide opportunities for them to enrich their vocabulary outside the classroom.

Chapter 5 looks at some commonly available software and examines the way that computers have become 'normalized' – a term used by Stephen Bax to describe a situation where technology is used so appropriately that it has become invisible. For example, in an English for Academic Purposes (EAP) context, learners compose texts for their lecturers without noticing the many benefits of being able to cut and paste text, or use a spell-checker to review and edit their work. The chapter also looks at the benefits of using software such as Microsoft PowerPoint, which is rapidly taking over from overhead projectors (OHPs) and becoming the norm for presentations.

Chapter 6 focuses on interactive whiteboards. Teachers who are lucky enough to teach using an interactive whiteboard are able to embed technology in their lessons in exciting ways. One teacher commented that the IWB has opened up her classroom to the real world. She uses the Internet wherever appropriate, and learners bring in the PowerPoint presentations they have prepared at home in order to show them to the class. This is very much a blended-learning scenario.

Chapter 7 looks at portable devices, such as Personal Digital Assistants (PDAs), digital audio recorders and camcorders. Teachers can create and distribute course materials which learners can access and respond to at a time and place convenient to them.

Chapter 8 looks at computer-mediated communication, or CMC. This refers to situations as diverse as communicating through the keyboard with penpals overseas, sending an email across the world, or making a telephone call across the Internet, using a system such as Skype™. The chapter covers the range of ways in which learners and teachers can communicate through the medium of the computer. It then describes the use of a Virtual Learning Environment (VLE) in language teaching. A group of learners at university may meet in class, and then communicate with each other informally through Chat; discuss the topic of their next lesson using a forum; email their tutor; and receive their course materials on their VLE. *Blended learning* is a term which is frequently applied to a situation when a course is delivered partly through F2F classes and partly through CMC (computer-mediated communication).

One logical extreme of integrating CMC tools in language teaching would be to run a course wholly online. It could be argued that in such a course, a teacher is present in many of the interactions, monitoring the interactions in a virtual classroom or answering emails. However, this book will not focus specifically on the role and skills of the purely online tutor, although some of these practices are mentioned in Chapter 8. In our definition of blended learning, we assume that teachers and learners meet in the classroom at some points during the course. An online tutor never meets the learners in person. For a detailed look at the methodology of online tutoring, there are a number of excellent books available. We particularly recommend *E-tivities* by Gilly Salmon (2002), which specifically focuses on online teaching.

Chapter 9 looks at creating your own materials. We will look at the way teachers communicate with their learners using blogs, and how learners can build up a sense of community and collaboration using a class wiki.

Chapter 10 concludes the book with a brief look at the future. Given the speed at which new technologies are developed, introduced and gain a myriad of uses, both intended and unexpected, the supporting website will keep you abreast of these exciting changes, and how they influence and affect language teaching.

Using technology in language teaching

Why use technology in language teaching? What opportunities does it offer? We believe that there are many. Firstly, using technology can be motivating. Playing language-learning games is one example of this, with learners enjoying tasks, and at the same time deriving learning benefits through recycling of language. Many learners simply like using the computer. They like multimedia exercises, as they can proceed at their own pace. They can make their own choices as to how to work through the materials.

Secondly, the 'interactivity' of language exercises can be highly beneficial. Web-based exercises are more interactive than paper-based exercises. This can appeal to many learners. Setting learners to work on an interactive exercise can add variety to the class. It offers them a chance to review language in a different way – perhaps doing a mix-and-match exercise game with collocations they have just learned.

Thirdly, the type of feedback which good interactive materials provide is appreciated by learners. They can get instant feedback on what they have done. Figure 1.1 shows an example of an interactive, online exercise from the Macmillan English Campus.

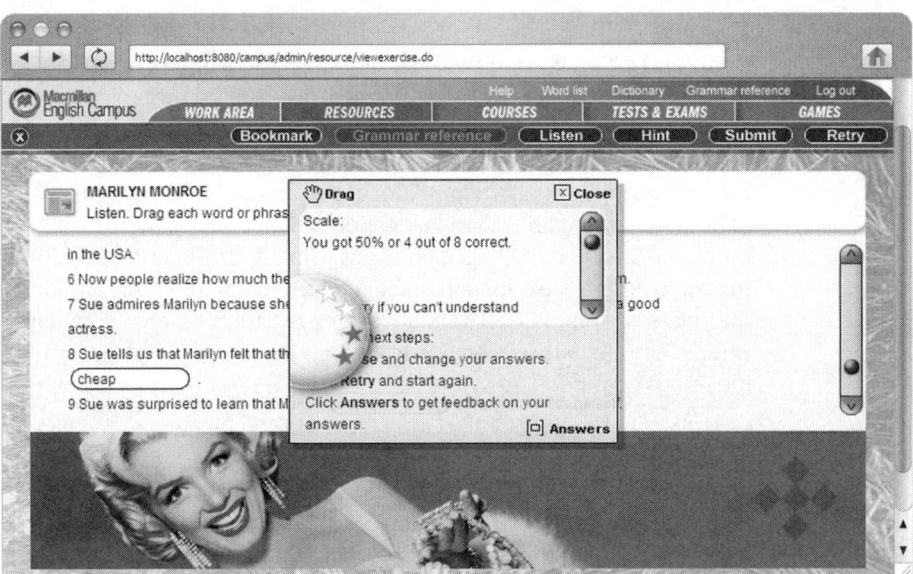

Figure 1.1
Language feedback
on web-based
exercises

Learners can see that they have scored, in the above example, 7 out of 9. This is also given in % terms. At this point, the user has three options:

[Close]	change their answers
[Retry]	clear their answers and start the exercise again
[Answers]	see which answers are correct and which are incorrect

The instant feedback offered by technology on exercises is usually perceived as helpful. Learners can make choices as to how many times they redo an exercise.

One of the great benefits mentioned earlier in this chapter relates to the opportunities afforded by CMC (computer-mediated communication). The computer is used to enable communication between two groups (teacher and learner, for instance) separated by time, distance or both. Supporting a course with technology can allow learners and teacher more flexibility in both time and place. Between classes, learners can access their materials whenever they want to. For example, EAP learners who take poor lecture notes can access the tutors' handouts on the VLE; this can have a dramatic effect on their revision, enabling them to complete their notes at a later date.

Learners today have high expectations when it comes to technology. Younger learners, the 'digital natives', are part of the Net generation and expect a language school to offer opportunities to use technology in their courses, for example via a well-equipped self-access centre. Business English learners practising giving a PowerPoint presentation expect to be videoed and to receive feedback from the teacher on their presentation skills as well as their English.

The use of technology outside the language classroom can make learners more autonomous. One key feature of using technology in learning is that it allows language practice and study away from the confines of the classroom. That could be in a hotel room, the office, an Internet café or, of course, at home. As learners become used to evaluating and selecting materials, they are able to plan out their own use of web-based materials in their own time. This helps them to become independent learners.

The use of technology can be time saving. Posting course materials online for learners to access can save the teacher the time and expense of photocopying. A teacher who prepares and saves a lesson in an interactive whiteboard can recycle the lesson with the next group, so any investment in preparation time can be made worthwhile. Of course, the time taken to become familiar with technology needs to be factored in, and this should not be underestimated. Nor should that obscure the benefits of teachers using a bank of shared electronic materials.

In addition, the use of technology can be current. Using a listening activity with today's news in the language classroom from a website such as the BBC's can add a dimension of immediacy to a lesson. This can supplement the traditional role of published materials, which tend to have a longer shelf life.

When we consider the role of technology, it is very helpful to distinguish between the language skills (reading, listening, writing, speaking). These have traditionally been divided into productive and receptive skills. Clearly, there are differences in the type of practice required to develop each of the four skills.

In the area of the receptive skills of listening and reading, it is possible to identify a clear role played by a web-based environment in providing exposure. Listening to digital audio, learners have the opportunity to pause at will, and listen and read a transcript. Reading on-screen, learners can access meaning on demand by clicking on a hyperlink to find out the meaning of a word.

The productive skills of speaking and writing are significantly different, in that the assessment of the output of speaking and writing activities does rely on human interpretation. Although writing is in a sense ideally matched with the keyboard, nevertheless we would prefer a free composition to be evaluated and graded by a teacher.

We would also wish for a teacher to evaluate and give language feedback on a discussion. Spelling and grammar checkers cannot replace teacher assessment (and will not pick up every error – see Chapter 5).

There are, as we all know, a number of concerns which are frequently expressed about using technology. Critics of computer-based interactive exercises argue that 'stimulus–response' activities such as mix-and-match, gap-fill and true/false activities are essentially boring. They are informed by behaviourist principles and fly in the face of more communicative approaches. The traditional role of computers in grammar has been disparagingly called 'drill and kill'. The types of feedback offered on many exercises are seen as limiting. Also, many teachers continue to have concerns about the reliability of technology.

While some of these fears may be genuine, there are clearly many benefits to be derived from integrating technology into teaching and learning. There are many factors which influence the extent to which teachers use technology in their courses. We will now look at some of these.

Factors influencing the uptake of blended learning

A number of important factors exist which will influence the use of technology in language courses. These include attitude, level, the volume and type of teacher training organized, your own and your learners' access to these resources, and cost.

Teachers and learners may hold positive, negative or neutral attitudes towards technology. Attitudes range across a spectrum or cline, from technophile to technophobic. Having a stance of 'healthy scepticism' is one approach to hearing about a new technology. In our view, it is equally important to be able to see the potential benefits.

The learners' level may be an influencing factor in which type of technology you use and how often it is used. One example is a low-level learner, reaching saturation point on a one-to-one course. You may decide to set this learner up on a CD-ROM to practise colours, numbers, days of the week or months of the year. The guided practice is a welcome break from the demands of the course, and provides review and consolidation.

Teacher training is a vital factor in the uptake of new technology. It is useful to consider which areas and knowledge are useful for teachers – what do you need to know today about the area of technology in ELT? We recommend that every teacher acquires a basic knowledge about using technology in ELT and skills to incorporate technology into their courses. These we term 'core skills'. Core skills include, for example, knowing which websites, interactive materials and useful CD-ROMs to recommend your learners, and how CD-ROM dictionaries work. In terms of skills, you should have the ability to search the Web efficiently, create a worksheet from text and pictures, and be able to evaluate materials downloaded from the Web and web-based exercises.

When you have acquired these core skills, there are many ways they can be extended: learning about interactive whiteboards and how to create PowerPoint presentations, for instance. Another useful skill is knowing how to link an electronic data projector to a laptop for an in-class presentation.

At an advanced level, you may wish to learn how to use tools for creating online materials or podcasts. You may wish to use course-building tools in a virtual learning environment, or use video-conferencing facilities.

Your own access to technology, and what access is available to your learners, is key to how it is incorporated in your courses. Computers are becoming more and more common in language teaching. The digital divide certainly exists, with some areas of education and some parts of the globe being well supplied with computers and interactive whiteboards, and other parts of the world with a low level of Internet access, or slow connection speeds. Nevertheless, common trends include a rise in broadband connections, more learners with access to computers both in school and at home, and more data projectors.

Finally, an obvious factor is cost. When a new technology is first developed and introduced onto the market, it may have a high cost. Consider the early days of the data projector or the first CD-ROMs. When a technology becomes popular and ubiquitous, costs fall. This issue is clearly an important factor influencing the uptake of, say, interactive whiteboards.

Having looked at some of the reasons for using technology in language teaching and learning, and some of the factors which contribute to its successful integration, we will conclude with some guiding principles which we would argue enable teachers to tap into the potential for 'blended learning'.

Balancing traditional approaches and technology

In our consideration of a blended-learning approach, we are guided by four key principles.

1 Separate the role of the teacher and the role of the technology

It is important to consider the respective roles of the teacher and technology. Although there may be areas of overlap, it is important not to see the teacher and technology as interchangeable and to clearly distinguish what each can do that the other cannot. In other words, we are not concerned that the teacher will be replaced by the computer because the teacher and the technology play different roles. Let us examine these.

The teacher is there to do a number of things which require human interaction: firstly, to perform a needs analysis. The teacher tests the learners and may also get to know them in terms of personality and attitude. He or she can be supported in this task by technology (an adaptive test on CD-ROM; an Excel spreadsheet; needs-analysis software to help placement, such as the *Business English Generator*), but, we would insist, not replaced by technology.

The teacher will then create the learning syllabus. Again, a computer may play a role in this (Office software, for instance), but decisions such as the choice of conversation topic are in the remit of the experienced professional. The teacher in the classroom writes the lesson plan and delivers the class. He or she will then interpret the materials, moderate the fluency sessions, react to learner utterances and so on. The teacher is there to deal with 'fuzzy' areas of language, to set and follow up 'free practice'. Language comprises both predictable and unpredictable elements. The number of possible utterances is potentially infinite, and the teacher needs to develop learners' ability to react to the unexpected, usually in a fluency classes.

Technology does some things better than the teacher – lightning-fast searches of an electronic dictionary is one example. The technology is available 24/7. It can offer endless exposure to the target language. The technology offers learners the possibility to control the exposure they receive – in a CD-ROM program, for example. Learners can pause an audio clip at will, play it as many times as they like, or redo an exercise until they feel satisfied with their result. This phenomenon has been described as the 'computer acting as workhorse'.

As we have outlined earlier in this chapter, the technology can offer limitless opportunities for 'guided practice' and consolidation. Learners can do lots of extra language practice outside the classroom. The computer does not get tired! Technology can give feedback on 'crisp' areas of language, such as grammar rules. There is clearly a role for computers in helping learners gain practice in using language in guided situations.

In a blended approach, we would separate the role of the teacher and the role of the technology. A blended approach sees the roles of teachers and technology as complementary. Artificial intelligence (AI) is not yet sufficiently developed to cope with real-world interactions in any but predictable exchanges, and there is no danger of it replacing the language teacher.

2 Teach in a principled way

Whenever a new technology appears, there is something which is called the 'wow' effect. However, we should not be seduced by the novelty, we should always focus on the learners' needs. We should ask ourselves whether the technology will improve teaching and enhance learning. We must ensure that the teaching is driven by the pedagogy and supported by the technology.

Occasionally, the technology may be used simply 'because it is there' – as in the case of a language game being played at the end of the day. Even in this situation, the teacher may be adding variety to the lesson, and allowing learners to consolidate the language.

3 Use technology to complement and enhance F2F teaching

The practical activities in this book assume that the technology in some ways complements and enhances a classroom activity. Learners may play a game which recycles language in a fun context. Similarly, integration is a key concept. If there is a close correlation between the content of the lesson and the online materials, the online material will be used more enthusiastically.

4 'It's not so much the program, more what you do with it' (Jones, 1986)

This famous observation was made a relatively long time ago in technological terms and it still, in our view, holds true. Let us look at three ways of using a CD-ROM. Firstly, a learner buys a complete English course on CD-ROM, sits at home and follows the course. We do not think this addresses the complex issues involved in learning a language. Speaking a language has a social dimension – we communicate with others. This particular use of the technology over-emphasizes the guided-practice element of language learning at the expense of real-time communication. Secondly, a CD-ROM can also complement a taught course. The teacher practises the present perfect tense using learner names, real-world examples and local context. There may be authentic interaction, clarification and restricted use of the language (Scrivener, 2005). Then, in the self-study period or at home, the learner consolidates using the exercises set by the teacher. This model of blended learning can be effective. Thirdly, a CD-ROM may be used in class as part of a presentation, using an electronic projector, in ways that the creators of the disk never envisaged when they wrote the exercise rubric. Here, it may be used in ways which promote communication between the learners.

In conclusion, we have seen that the term *blended learning* can have a range of meanings. We have defined it as referring to a language course which combines a F2F (face-to-face) classroom component with an appropriate use of technology. We have suggested that the technology can be integrated into the language lessons, or be used by learners outside the classroom for further practice, and to complement the taught element of the course.

The World Wide Web consists of a vast network of electronic 'pages' which hold information in the form of text, pictures, audio and video. These web pages are stored on millions of interconnected computers and other electronic storage devices worldwide and are grouped together into 'sites'. While the terms are often used interchangeably, the term 'Internet' actually refers to the interconnected hardware that stores and carries the Web and other information.

The idea for the Web was proposed and put into action in the late eighties and early nineties by Sir Tim Berners-Lee, who was working at the CERN research facility in Switzerland. His idea was the hyperlink, which became the basis of the Web. Pages on the Web contain hyperlinks which point towards other web pages. When you click on a link with your mouse, you are instructing your computer to go and find the web page, audio clip, video clip, etc identified by that link. If the page identified by a link no longer exists, or has been renamed or moved, the connection fails. This is called a 'dead link'.

It was decided to make the technology of the Web free, allowing it to be used by anyone with the appropriate equipment and connection. As a result, the Web has grown exponentially since the mid-nineties. The number of websites runs into tens of millions and the number of web pages at over a billion.

This chapter is divided into four sections. The first will equip you with searching skills, or develop the skills you have, to help you find what you want from the Web. The second will discuss some ways of using that material as part of a blended-learning language course. The last two sections will provide some practical ideas which you can incorporate into your teaching and look at some examples where this has been applied.

How to find materials

Finding websites

Searching efficiently, or 'smart searching', consists of knowing how to sift through the millions of accessible web pages in the fastest and most effective way to find what you and your learners need. The best way to find something on the Web is to use a search engine.

At the time of writing, the three most popular search engines are:

Google   http://www.google.com
Yahoo   http://search.yahoo.com
MSN   http://search.msn.com

Their basic operation is very simple: you enter your search criteria in the form of words which describe the information you are searching for. The search engine produces a list of web pages whose content in some way fits those criteria.

Each search engine searches a different number of web pages and interprets the search criteria differently. Web pages or websites that appear at the top of a result list do not do so by chance. They are a combination of the most popular ones covering this topic and those whose owners have paid to appear near the top of the list when certain words are searched for. Remember that search engines only look for the things you tell them to look for: the more specific your search criteria, the more likely the results will include something useful to you.

The following pieces of basic advice can help you find what you want quickly:

- The more words in your search criteria, the smaller the number of results.
- Do not bother with capital letters and small words such as *the, in, and*, etc, since most search engines ignore them.
- If you cannot find something you want in the first 30–50 results, rethink your search criteria. Maybe add or remove words.
- Local versions of search engines are programmed to prioritize results from your country. For example, if you are based in the UK try using http://www.google.co.uk or http://uk.search.yahoo.com.

Once you have mastered the basics, further techniques can be added to improve your search results:

- Placing the + symbol in front a word means that this word must be on the web page for it to be included in the results.
- Placing a – symbol in front of a word means that no web pages with this word must be included in the results.
- Placing an OR between two words means the web pages must include either one of these words or both.
- Placing a phrase inside double quotation marks tells the search engine to look for this exact phrase.

Here are a few more tips that are unique to Google, the most popular of the search engines:

- Placing the ~ symbol in front of a word means Google should search for this word and synonyms of this word, eg *nuclear ~power* produces results for nuclear power, nuclear energy and nuclear electricity.
- You can limit your search to a single website instead of the entire Web. Your search criteria should be followed by *site*: then the address of the website, eg "*nuclear power*" *site:www.bbc.co.uk* will search for the term *nuclear power,* but only in the BBC's website.
- Google has a feature that allows you to limit your search to online glossaries. You enter *define*: followed by the word you want to know the meaning of, eg *define: nuclear power* produces a short list of definitions of nuclear power taken from specialized websites.
- Google News, http://news.google.com, searches only websites of news-gathering organizations such as newspapers and TV companies. Its homepage is generated automatically, and you can enter search criteria to find exactly what you are looking for. Because Google News only covers a very small part of the Web, it is able to list articles that are very recent, sometimes only a few hours old.

Finding multimedia

Multimedia on the Web consists of images – such as photographs and diagrams – audio and video. The latter range from clips of longer recordings to complete radio programmes, songs and TV programmes or movies. Texts are the most common things on the Web, with pictures coming second and audio and video following. This means that while it is often possible to find a text that exactly matches your needs, finding audio or video clips that fit closely is not guaranteed.

Images

Most search engines have special tools for finding images. At the homepage of each search engine, click on the link *Images* or use one of these addresses:

- Google images: http://www.google.com/imghp
- Yahoo images: http://search.yahoo.com/images
- MSN images: http://search.msn.com/images

When you search, instead of a list of web pages, you get a set of pictures that meet your criteria. If the results do not include what you were looking for, try modifying your search criteria.

Audio and video

The Web can expand the range of listening materials you have available to your learner in terms of content, length, accent, speed of speech and regional type of English.

There are some audio files which you can download, save and keep. To find out about these, see *Podcasts* on pages 20–21. Here, we are talking about streamed audio and video, which means sound and video pictures that are delivered to your computer as they are played, rather like radio or television. This requires you to be connected to the Internet for the duration of the playback.

Broadband Internet connections can cope with online video easily. However, slower connections will struggle to download the information quickly enough, so video is best avoided. Audio clips, however, require less bandwidth and are usually accessible with the slower, dial-up type of connection.

The two most common programs used to access streaming audio and video on Windows computers are RealPlayer and Windows Media Player. The latter comes pre-installed with Microsoft Windows on PCs. RealPlayer can be downloaded from http://www.real.com.

The RealPlayer interface is very user friendly. You can use the slider to 'rewind' the recording in order to listen again.

In order to search for audio clips, you need to use specialised audio search engines such as http://audio.search.yahoo.com and http://www.altavista.com/audio. Yahoo's search tool is mainly intended for finding pop songs. You enter search criteria and click on Audio Search. The results page defaults to 'music'. However, you can click on Podcasting or Other Audio to find results that are more likely to be spoken word. Clicking on links from Altavista's search results takes you directly to the web page the audio clip originated from, and then you are left to find the correct link to start the clip.

Searching for video is very similar to the audio search tools described above. Go to http://video.search.yahoo.com, http://www.altavista.com/video and http://video.google.com.

Other ways of finding material

You can also find information on the Web without searching. Search engines are a *pull* technology in which you, the user, go looking for what you need. Searching tends to be done as and when you need certain, specific information. The opposite of pull technology is *push* technology, which is when information is sent to you. Two of the items covered in this section are push technologies: email newsletters and RSS (Really Simple Syndicate). The others, blogs and podcasts, sometimes make use of push technology in addition to pull technology.

Push technologies are activated by the user. An email newsletter or an RSS feed is something you voluntarily subscribe to and can unsubscribe from. This is different from unsolicited email, otherwise known as *spam*.

Blogs

The name *blog* is a shortened form of *web log*. Blogs are defined most simply as online diaries. They consist of a website to which an author or authors, known as *bloggers*, contribute written postings, which can include pictures and sometimes audio and video clips. These are arranged in chronological order and automatically archived so that a blog can be searched for earlier entries than those displayed. Most importantly, many bloggers search the Web to pursue their own areas of interest and then include hyperlinks to the things that interest them in their postings. A standard feature of blogs is the opportunity for readers to respond. Many blog owners will allow readers to add comments to the blog postings and, on some blogs, these can develop into extended discussions or arguments.

In Chapter 9, we talk about how you can use blogs with your learners or to support your classes. Here, we are considering them as a source of information, opinions and links to other websites. This is because there are many blogs that focus on very specific topics. Finding good blogs that cover a topic of interest to you can save a lot of searching.

Blogs can be divided into a number of basic categories in terms of content and intended audience:

- **The diary:** These tend to have a single author who muses on his/her life and experiences. Many are mundane and not intended to be read by anyone other than the blogger's close family and friends. Others are intended for wider consumption and are read by an international audience.
- **The special interest blog:** Whatever the topic, there will be someone blogging on it and linking to other people writing and blogging about it.
- **The news blog:** These recycle stories reported on the Web, are often controversial or political in their stance, and occasionally throw up a major story which has been overlooked by the traditional media such as newspapers and television.
- **The technical blog:** These are operated by people in the IT community and are used as ways of sharing and commenting on ideas and developments.
- **The political blog:** These often have multiple authors and act as a forum for debates and discussions on political and occasionally philosophical topics.
- **The business blog:** These are maintained by companies as part of their web marketing strategy to provide customer information, response to customer feedback or just to give a sense that a business's website is up to date.

As with all things on the Web, the number of active blogs is overwhelming. In order to find useful and interesting blogs, it is best to use a specialist search engine. Here are three:

- Google Blog Search: http://blogsearch.google.com
- Blog Search Engine: http://www.blogsearchengine.com
- Ice Rocket: http://www.icerocket.com

The most serious and prolific bloggers often have email newsletters and/or RSS feeds.

Email newsletters

Email newsletters are very similar to their paper forebears. Many websites which offer them have regularly updated content, and the newsletter describes this new content so you do not have to remember to visit the site every day or week. Subscribing is usually as simple as providing your email address. When you subscribe, it is now a common practice for you to be sent an email asking you to confirm your wish to receive the newsletter. This is a security measure and prevents other people from signing you up for newsletters you do not want.

There are several styles of email newsletters:

- **The update newsletter:** These notify subscribers of new information on the main website and provide links to that information. They are also used by traditional broadcasters, such as TV channels, to announce what is coming up in the next programme, eg the nightly news.
- **The links newsletter:** As mentioned above, many bloggers search the web for links to material related to their interests. This type of newsletter provides a collection of those links.
- **The traditional newsletter:** This is more or less self-contained, with complete articles and photographs.
- **The marketing newsletter:** These are used by businesses to advertise their products and services and new promotions or competitions.

Remember that email newsletters are different from spam. Spam is unsolicited email, and there are many email filtering tools which are designed to block it before it arrives in your email inbox. If you subscribe to an email newsletter and you subsequently decide you no longer wish to receive it, you should click on the unsubscribe link that appears at the bottom of most newsletters and follow the procedure that notifies the sender of the newsletter. Blocking email newsletters you no longer want using a spam filter, especially with an online email service, may result in that email newsletter being blocked to other users of that email service, many of whom may wish to receive it.

RSS feeds

Subscribing to a Really Simple Syndication (RSS) feed allows you to keep track of the content of your favourite websites without having to visit them regularly. To use these, you require a program called an RSS Reader, into which you import the address of a website's RSS feed. You can then set the RSS Reader to check this feed at regular intervals. If there are any updates, the RSS Reader will automatically display a headline and a link. When you click on the link, the web page with that story will open in your browser. Most news websites use RSS. It is also common on blogs that are updated regularly.

The following RSS readers are available for free:

- Juice: http://www.kbcafe.com/juice/download.html
- GreatNews: http://www.curiostudio.com/download.html

Podcasts

The name *podcast* is a combination of Apple's well-known audio player, the iPod, and the word *broadcast* from TV and radio. A podcast is a computer audio file. The most common file format is mp3, which has a very good compression ratio, resulting in smaller file sizes and therefore shorter download times. However, other formats are occasionally used.

Podcasts are generally compared to radio programmes. They vary in length, content, style and quality. Some are aimed at general audiences, while others may be of interest to the tiniest fraction of those using the Web.

A podcast can be listened to in a variety of ways. Usually the entire file is downloaded and stored on a computer's hard drive. It can then be played through the computer's speakers or transferred to a portable music player, such as an iPod, and listened to anytime and anywhere. Note that, in practical terms, you need a broadband Internet connection to download a podcast. For example, a 30-minute podcast in mp3 format is a 13Mb file. The time required to download this with a dial-up connection could be measured in hours.

In your search for suitable authentic listening material, podcasts have a number of advantages over streaming audio. Once they have been downloaded, they can be kept and distributed by email, CD-ROM, mp3 players or other portable devices (see Chapter 7 for more details). Also, compared to older forms of audio media, such as audio cassettes, podcasts can be copied repeatedly without any loss of quality because they are digital files.

Podcasts come in a number of formats, including:

- **presentations:** pre-scripted and well organized
- **monologues:** a single person usually extemporising (or rambling, depending on your point of view!)
- **interviews:** a presenter asking guests questions
- **dialogues:** two or more people engaged in a conversation, usually about a pre-determined topic
- a combination of some or any of the above
- excerpts or a montage of excerpts from radio programmes – the best examples of these come from the BBC.

The following directory websites list podcasts by topic:

- Podcast.net: http://www.podcast.net
- Podcast.com: http://www.podcast.com
- iPodder: http://www.ipodder.org
- The Podcast Bunker: http://www.podcastbunker.com
- Yahoo! Podcasts: http://podcasts.yahoo.com

    This is part of the Yahoo web directory that specializes in podcasts or podcast websites. Each listed podcast has been rated by previous users using a star system.

A relatively recent development is the video podcast. These are not yet served by the same directory infrastructure, so are not as easy to find. At the time of writing, the most promising video podcasts were those produced by established news organizations, such as the BBC or other TV stations such as ABC in the USA. Since they contain both audio and video, video podcasts can be very large files with correspondingly long download times.

Opportunities and issues

Using authentic texts

One of the benefits of the Web is the ability to easily access authentic material. Such material can be of great value for discussion classes, debates or project work in which learners need to explore the controversy surrounding a topic. It can also be useful when the learners' needs are very specific, fall outside of the range of published materials or simply need to be authentic and current.

Once you have located a text that you want to use with your learners, it can be copied from the web page and into a word-processor document. Do this by highlighting it with your cursor in the same way you would in a word-processor program. Then right-click with your mouse and select Copy, or press the *Ctrl* key (⌘ on Macs) and the letter *C* on your keyboard. Finally, open a new word-processor document and click on the Paste button, or *Ctrl* and *V* on the keyboard. You can now save the text and edit it to create material to use with your learners.

The types of activities you can do are those often used in reading lessons. The following list gives examples of common modifications to texts to create activities:

- Separating the headlines from the text as a predicting exercise.
- Simplifying the text to remove or replace vocabulary and idiomatic language you think will distract from the target of your lesson or is inappropriate for your learners' level.
- Creating a gap-fill exercise by editing out target language or structures.
- Creating an exercise to match sub-headlines with paragraphs.
- Putting paragraphs or sentences onto separate pages to be put back into the correct order.
- Selecting a short passage to use as a dictation or dictagloss (reconstructing a text from memory, usually in pairs) exercise.

As well as using the Web as a source of texts to adapt, you can encourage computer-literate learners to find, choose and modify texts themselves to use in the classroom. See the practical applications at the end of this chapter for an example.

Using multimedia materials

Pictures and photographs have many uses in the classroom, especially with lower levels. You can use them to teach vocabulary, prompt discussions and support activities such as presentations. Like texts, images can be copied and pasted into word-processor documents or incorporated into presentation slides. They can be used to create flashcards and added to vocabulary exercises.

The principal benefits of online audio and video start with the range of material in terms of subject matter, accent of the speaker and length. It is a characteristic of the Web that someone somewhere is recording material about almost any conceivable topic. Learners who require exposure to native-speaker accents other than those in their immediate environment can listen online. Audio and video available on the Web currently range from clips that are less than a minute for news reports to continuous live radio and TV from around the world. If you have access to the Web, then these listening opportunities are always available. The final major benefit is currency: whether you are looking for pop videos, news reports or press conferences, the latest will be available on the Web.

As with searching for texts and images above, finding appropriate and interesting listening material can be done by both you and your learners. Learners with access to the Web at home or work can be encouraged to integrate listening into their everyday routines.

If you have searched for and selected an online audio or video clip you intend to use with your learners, then you are able to prepare in advance of the lesson and use the recording in a similar way to published materials, ie pre-teach vocabulary, use listening tasks for gist then detail.

However, the use of online listening material as part of a language course can differ from using traditional published material. If learners have been tasked with finding their own listening or are using an online news service with up-to-the-minute reports, then you will not be able to prepare supporting material, such as comprehension questions, in advance. This moves the emphasise from teacher-led activities onto learner training. You should prepare your learners to be as proactive as possible. They can independently check their understanding against another source. In the case of a news report, the website of the news service will also have a written account of the story against which the learners' understanding of the audio version can be compared. You can also show your learners how to use listening material for collecting vocabulary and as an aid to improving their pronunciation.

Often learners like to have transcripts of the material they are listening to. This is also an aid and motivation for learners who are working independently. A few websites provide full transcripts for authentic audio recordings. As before, you should encourage your learners to be proactive in their use of these transcripts. Suggest that they listen without the text first before reading to check their understanding. Try the following:

- BBC Learning English – Words in the News: http://www.bbc.co.uk/worldservice/learningenglish/newsenglish
  For detailed information about this website, see Chapter 3.

- Australian Broadcasting Company – World Today programme:
  http://www.abc.net.au/worldtoday
  Regular news reports from Australia, often including interviews.

Podcasts can be used in similar ways to streaming audio and video. The main difference is the fact they can be downloaded and stored. This means that you can find and select podcasts to use with your learners and prepare material such as comprehension questions, vocabulary sheets, etc. Since podcasts are portable, easily distributable and can be played on a variety of devices, listening activities can be set as homework. As with blogs, learners can be encouraged to find podcasts that meet their interests or language needs and start to download and listen to them on a regular basis.

Another benefit of audio in digital format is the ability to quickly locate an exact position in a recording. With magazine-style podcasts, such as those from the Guardian Unlimited website (see page 34), you can make a note of counter timings as you are listening in preparation for using the recording. You can instruct learners to go to the exact position in the podcast where the discussion or report you wish to focus on begins, as well as tell them where it ends. This allows for listening activities that are of a specific length. The learners know how long they are going to listen for, and you are able, if you wish, to prepare specific comprehension questions on the chosen segment.

Regular updates

The main opportunity offered by blogs to learners is reading material. If you or your learners find a blog or blogs that are of interest either personally or, in the case of learners who are improving their language skills for their job, professionally, then they can provide a motivation for regular contact with the language. Clearly a balance needs to be found between the learners' independence to choose and the quality of the language used on the blog. Not all blogs are written by native speakers of the language they are using, and not all native speakers are able to produce consistently accurate written language. See *Practical activities* (page 32) for an activity which addresses this issue.

If you work in an ESP area which requires you to stay up to date with your learners' subject matter, or you often require material that focuses on new developments, then newsletters can cut out a lot of searching. They are equally useful for the learners in question to stay up to date with their area and the language involved. Newsletters also have the benefit of being a push technology; the learner does not have to make time to go and find information – it is delivered to their in-box on a regular basis. Some examples include:

- MarketingProfs.com: http://www.marketingprofs.com
  A website dedicated to all things related to marketing for the Business English teacher.
- Hieros Gamos: http://www.hierosgamos.org
  If you teach English for law, then this website's newsletter will keep you up to date on any legal topic you care to name.

The main opportunity associated with RSS (see page 20) is keeping track of a large number of potential sources of online information without having to visit each website individually and at regular intervals. As a teacher sourcing authentic texts and audio and video clips, this makes your life a lot easier. This is especially the case if you have a number of websites which you regard as reliable sources of material. RSS software allows you to specify which websites you wish to keep track of and how often you want to check for new content. You can label or bookmark interesting stories to use at a later date.

RSS software can be used in activities with learners which involve searching. If you want your learners to search for a text or audio/video clip but prefer to limit them to certain websites, you can use an RSS program that has been set up to collect feeds from only those websites.

Search activities

Search engines such as Google can be used for a range of activities, both for finding information and for testing out hypotheses about the language. Some of these are detailed in the *Practical activities* section on pages 27–31.

Webquests

Webquests are research activities that require learners to collect information about a subject using the Web. They have been used for teaching children for many years, especially in the USA, where Internet access has been more common than other parts of the world. Webquests are also used in language teaching. The exercise is written in the target language, as are the online resources the learners use to find the required information, as well as the result of the activity, whether it is written or presented verbally. The searching for suitable online resources is done beforehand by the teacher, and those websites form an integral part of the activity.

Webquests are generally divided into five parts:

1 **Introduction:** This sets the scene and gives some background to the task. Learners are sometimes given roles.

2 **Task:** A general explanation of the webquest is given so that learners know what the target is and what sort of outcome is expected.

3 **Process:** This is the set of instructions which give the steps required to achieve the target. It also includes the resources which are the links to websites where the information required to complete the task can be found.

4 **Evaluation:** This outlines how the learners' performance in the task will be accessed. For language learners, this will include an assessment of the English they have produced, as well as how well they completed the task.

5 **Conclusion:** This final stage explains what learners should have got out of doing the webquest. In the case of language learners, it might be the acquisition of new vocabulary, an opportunity to review or practise some area of grammar, or finding information or material for a discussion or role-play.

There are a growing number of teachers creating webquests for their language learners and posting them on websites. If you decide to create your own, it is a good idea to search for and look at some of these to get an idea of how they are constructed, worded and the kinds of tasks they feature. As your web-searching skills improve, so will the resources you are able to provide your learners as part of a webquest. You can also use the template on page 135.

In any discussion on the use and adaptation of authentic materials, it is important to mention copyright. The rules for copyright on anything published on the Web are as stringent as those for materials published and distributed in other ways, eg books, newspapers, TV, CDs, etc.

Practical activities

Authentic texts

Authentic text gap-fill

Aim: to create a gap-fill exercise using an authentic text from the Web

Level: intermediate to advanced

Interaction: pairwork

Technology: search engine and word processor

Rationale: It is very straightforward to find a text on the Web, copy it into a word-processor document, then remove words to create a gap-fill exercise. This activity hands that process to the learners.

Before class: This activity works best if you have previously created and used similar material with your learners so that they are familiar with the concept. If you have also done the 'Brainstorming search criteria' activity below, they will already be familiar with the process of searching for a text.

Procedure:

1 The whole class brainstorms a topic they would like to focus on. They also discuss and agree on the type of language they are going to remove to make their gap-fill exercises, eg prepositions, verbs, etc. Finally, they agree on whether or not to include the missing words as part of the exercise.

2 At the computer, they work in pairs to search and find a text on the agreed topic.

3 They copy that text into a word-processor document and replace some words with a gap using underscore symbols, ie _____ . If it has been agreed to include the missing words, these should be retyped at the top of the page.

4 If there is no access to the Web where the class is being held, stages 2 and 3 can be set as homework, with the subsequent stage carried out the next time the class meets.

5 The completed gap-fill exercises are printed and distributed to other members of the group, who try to complete the exercise.

Note: An expanded version of these instructions appears on page 134 if you want to provide a handout for learners.

Multimedia materials

American accents

Aim: to provide exposure to American accents

Level: intermediate to advanced

Interaction: pairwork

Technology: search engine and media player

Rationale: The Web provides opportunities to find and listen to a wide variety of different accents. In this activity, the learners also have the motivation of choosing their own audio clip. The following procedure is aimed at teenage learners, but could be used with or adapted for adults.

Before class: As always, try this one yourself so you know how it works. If you have access to the Web where you teach, you should also provide the learners with a demonstration of the search procedure with the Altavista audio search.

Procedure:

1 The class brainstorms their favourite American movie or pop stars and agree on two, eg one male and one female.

2 The class is divided into pairs and given a copy of the worksheet (page 137).

3 At the computer, each pair goes to the Altavista audio search. They enter the word *interview* and the name of the actor or pop star. From the list, they find an interview that is about five minutes long.

4 They listen to the interview and prepare a report on the contents to present to the rest of the class.

5 The class reconvenes and each pair presents their findings.

News reports

Aim: to listen to a news report on a relevant topic

Level: intermediate to advanced

Interaction: individual

Technology: search engine and media player

Rationale: The BBC's news website provides access to an extensive archive of video clips from BBC news programmes. This archive can be searched using a standard text-entry search box. All the reports are by native speakers. This activity works well with Business English learners; the search criteria could then be as simple as 'car industry' or 'oil industry'. The following procedure is intended for a one-to-one course, but could be adapted for larger groups.

Before class: If you are going to propose a subject to the learner, try the search before the class to make sure that there is a choice of appropriate clips available. If your search does not produce any good results straight away, modify your search criteria.

Procedure:

1 Introduce your learner to the BBC news website. Click on a Watch link to demonstrate the video clips.

2 Explain about the video-clip archive.

3 Enter your search criteria in the search box at the top of the news homepage.

4 On the results page, direct your learner towards the 'BBC Audio & Video' button at the top. Demonstrate how to get more results by clicking on the 'more results' link at the bottom of the list.

5 From the list, agree which ones you are both going to listen to.

6 Give the learner time to listen and, if necessary, take notes. Remind him/her that he/she can pause the report and go back and listen to parts again if necessary.

7 Listen to the selected reports yourself.

8 After the agreed time, compare notes with the learner about what he/she has understood.

Follow on: Any discussion that arises from the content of the news reports can be pursued as a fluency activity.

Search-engine activities

Brainstorming search criteria

Aim: to search the Web to find a text on an agreed topic

Level: elementary to advanced

Interaction: whole class, pairwork, individual

Technology: search engine

Rationale: Learners' motivation to read and study an authentic text is increased if they have had some input in choosing the text. Here, they are searching for a text on an agreed topic which will be used by the entire class. It can be done as a whole-class activity with lower levels or with the class divided into pairs or small groups for more advanced learners.

Procedure:

1 The class agrees on a topic.

2 In pairs, the learners brainstorm ten words they think will feature in the text.

3 Once the pairs have their ten words, they test them with an agreed search engine. Create a limit such as 'The text must come from a webpage in the first 30 results'.

4 If there is no access to the Web where the class is being held, the searching stage can be set as homework, with the subsequent stages carried out the next time the class meets.

5 The learners print the text they have selected and prepare to say why it should be chosen by the class.

6 The class reconvenes, each pair presents its texts and the class votes to choose which one to use.

Follow on: You can use the chosen text in a number of ways, such as reading comprehension or vocabulary development, or as a lead-in to a class discussion on the topic.

Collocation finder

Aim: to investigate common collocations for a word

Level: intermediate and higher

Interaction: pairwork

Technology: search engine

Rationale: When a search engine lists its results, it presents a short piece of text from each web page listed. These can yield some interesting collocations. However, it can also be a very hit-and-miss affair.

Before class: Select a few words you wish your learners to investigate and test them in a search engine before starting. The Google news search is especially good for this. As a test, try the word *power* and see how many collocations you can note down from the first 30 results.

Procedure:

1 Give your learners the words you want them to investigate and tell them which search engine they should use. You could assign different search engines to different pairs to add an extra variable to the activity.

2 Before they go to the computers, ask learners to brainstorm as many collocations as they can think of and make a list. They can use the worksheet at the back of the book (page 138).

3 At the computer, the learners have a time limit to find as many collocations as they can.

4 If there is no access to the Web where the class is being held, the searching stage can be set as homework, with the subsequent stages carried out the next time the class meets.

5 After searching, the learners compare the collocations they have found. They can use a learner's dictionary to check any that they are not confident about.

Follow-on: Make sure you then give your learners opportunities to recycle the collocations in fluency activities.

Grammar checker

Aim: to check the understanding of a grammar keyword

Level: advanced

Interaction: pairwork

Technology: search engine

Rationale: The short piece of text from each web page listed in a search engine's results can be used to check the use of a grammar keyword.

Before class: Select the keywords you wish your learners to investigate and test them in the search engines you intend your learners to use. The Google news search is especially good for this activity. As a test, try the word *may* and see how many examples you can note down from the first 30 results which demonstrate its uses for giving permission and talking about future possibility.

Procedure:

1 Give your learners the keywords you want them to investigate and tell them which search engine you want them to use. You could assign different search engines to different pairs.

2 Before they go to the computers, ask the learners to note down what they think the keyword is used for and give at least one example sentence for each use.

3 At the computer, the learners have a time limit to search for other sentences that confirm their idea about the keyword's use or to add to or modify that idea.

4 If there is no access to the Web where the class is being held, the searching stage can be set as homework, with the subsequent stages carried out the next time the class meets.

5 After searching, the learners compare their results. They can use a grammar text to check any that they are not confident about.

Follow-on: You can return to previous mistakes your learners have made with the keywords they tested and ask them to correct these mistakes in the light of any new information they have acquired. As always, it is important to give your learners the opportunity to use the target language in a fluency activity.

Collocation tester

Aim: to test collocations

Level: intermediate to advanced

Interaction: pairwork

Technology: search engine (Google)

Rationale: This uses the 'exact phrase' search feature of search engines to test the frequency of use of correct and incorrect collocations.

Before class: Choose a number of collocation mistakes that your learners have made recently or make persistently. This can be done by using your notes or feedback sheets from previous fluency activities. Alternatively, you can prepare a sheet of common mistakes, such as the use of *make* and *do*. The activity works by putting quotation marks around the collocations your learners are testing and making a note of the number of results displayed at the top of the screen. As an example, try *make mistake* and *do mistake*. The correct collocation will produce a considerably larger number of results than the incorrect one.

Procedure:

1 Give your learners a list of correct and incorrect collocations.

2 Before they go to the computer, ask them which they think are which.

3 Explain how to use the 'exact phrase' search feature on Google

4 At the computers, the learners search for each collocation, make a note of the number of results and decide which collocations are correct.

5 If there is no access to the Web where the class is being held, the searching stage can be set as homework, with the subsequent stages carried out the next time the class meets.

6 The class reconvenes, and pairs compare their results. If any of the results are inconclusive, learners can use a dictionary to find the correct answer.

Follow on: Make sure you then give your learners opportunities to recycle the collocations in fluency activities.

Variation: This procedure can also be applied to grammatical structures such as *I'm agree* and *I agree* (see Figure 2.1) or to compare the use of correct structures such as *I work for* and *I'm working for.*

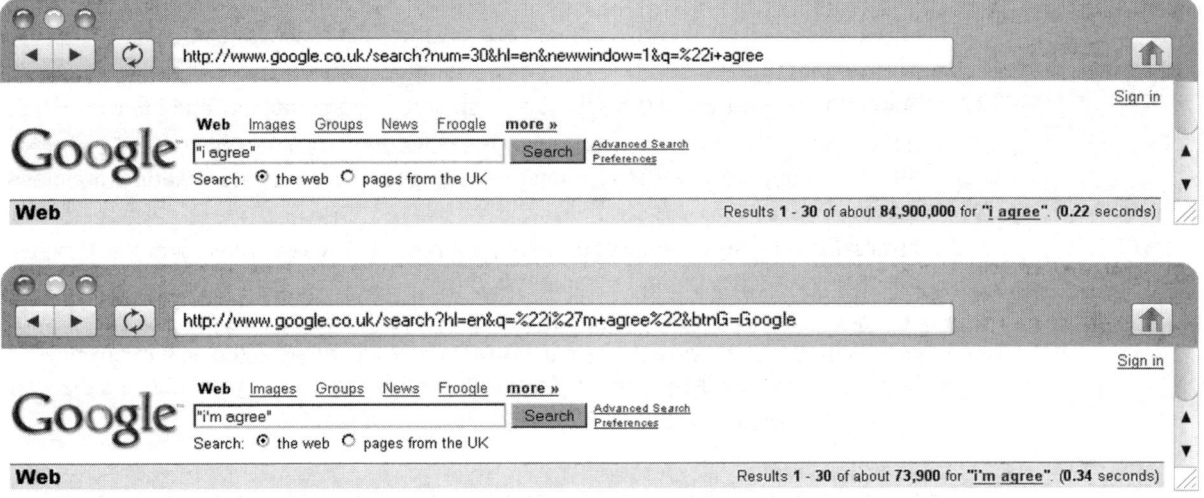

Figure 2.1

The Google search results for "i'm agree" and "i agree".

Note the number of results for each one.

London visit webquest (see pages 24–25)

Aim: to perform a webquest

Level: intermediate

Interaction: pairwork / small groups

Technology: browser

Rationale: Webquests are self-contained activities that require learners to access specified websites, collect information and report back their findings using the target language. They can revolve around imaginary situations or be linked to a real-world task. The London visit webquest may be an imaginary situation for many learners, but could be adapted for a group of learners who are planning a real visit to London.

Before class: As with all activities that use links to websites, check that they are live before using them with a group of learners.

Procedure:

1 Ask the class if anyone has been to London before and if so, what they saw and what they would recommend. If there is anyone who would like to visit London or is planning to visit, ask what they would most like to see.

2 Distribute the 'London visit webquest' worksheet to the class (see page 136). Ask learners to read the introduction and confirm that everyone understands what the timeframe is.

3 Ask them to read the task and confirm that they are to visit three famous landmarks, one big museum and do some shopping. Make sure that they are aware that they need to consider how much money they will have to spend and that they need to think about travelling around the city and the time that will take.

4 Ask the learners to read the process. Confirm that everybody is clear that the task is to produce a rough timetable for the day based on the interests of the pair or small group they are working in.

5 Divide the class into pairs or small groups; allocate a computer to each group. Set a period of time for doing the online research (approximately 20 minutes) and preparing the timetables (approximately 15 minutes). Before they start researching, ask them to read the evaluation criteria and remind them that it is the language they use in presenting their timetable that is going to assessed.

6 If computer resources are not available, the research stage of this activity can be set as homework to be done individually and the presentation of the timetables done when the class next meets

7 The learners each present their timetables for the day. You can provide language feedback after, particularly on the language for talking about future plans, which is the grammar focus of this webquest.

Blogs and podcasts

Comparing blogs

Aim: to compare the blogs that members of a class have chosen to read

Level: intermediate to advanced

Interaction: individual then class

Technology: browser

Rationale: Regularly reading a blog which covers an interesting topic is good for reading practice and vocabulary development. However, not all blogs provide good, accurate models of the language.

Before class: Select one or two blogs to use as examples if your learners are not familiar with the idea.

Procedure:

This activity is in three steps over a period of time:

1 **Finding a blog:** Introduce the concept of a blog to class members who do not know what they are. Explain that each member of the class is going to search for and find a blog that they plan to read regularly outside of class time. Show the class how to use a blog search engine and brainstorm subjects that might be of interest to individual members of the class. Set the task for each member to find a blog and start reading it regularly for an agreed period, eg two weeks.

2 **Reading the blog:** The members of the group search for and find a blog and read it each day for the agreed period. They also start to prepare to present the blog to the rest of the class.

3 **Accessing the blog:** After the agreed period, each member of the class presents the blog they have been reading. They need to say why it is (or, perhaps, is not) interesting, and provide examples of postings. Other members of the class can ask questions, and the samples are examined for the accuracy of the language they use. If it becomes apparent that any of the blogs being read are using limited or incorrect language, the person who chose it can defend it, agree to choose another, or pick from the blogs presented by the other class members.

Follow on: With ongoing classes, this activity can be repeated at regular intervals, with class members presenting the most interesting postings from the blog they are reading, as well as any new and useful vocabulary they have learned from the blog.

Podcasts for self-study

Aim: to choose and listen to podcasts outside of the classroom

Level: intermediate to advanced

Interaction: individual

Technology: podcast and portable digital audio player

Rationale: Mp3 audio files can be played on a variety of devices such as mobile phones and PDAs, as well as media players (see Chapter 7 for details). Many learners already download music from the Web and listen to it on these types of devices. Introducing them to podcasts with spoken content which they can listen to outside the classroom does not involve a major shift in behaviour.

Before class: Check that all your learners do, in fact, have some sort of device which can play mp3 files and that they know how to download mp3s from the Web and then transfer them to those devices.

Procedure:

1 Brainstorm topics of interest with the entire class.

2 Introduce the class to Podcast.net and provide time for your learners to search and find podcasts on those topics.

3 The learners report back on the podcasts they have found. If you have a group of younger learners, this is now the time to exercise a decision about whether the content of the podcasts is appropriate for that age group.

4 Each learner is allocated a podcast to download, listen to and evaluate. They can use the worksheet at the back of the book (page 139).

5 After an agreed period, each learner reports back to the class and gives his/her evaluation of the podcast. Podcasts should be evaluated on the basis of how interesting the content is, how easy or difficult the speakers are to understand, and the sound quality of recording.

Follow on: The class can then select one of the podcasts that they will all listen to as homework to discuss in a future lesson.

Case studies

Case study 1:
Integrating blogs and RSS readers in a specialized course

Samantha is based in-company at a computer firm where she teaches senior management, sales staff and software engineers. They all need to be up to date with the fast-changing world of information technology. She has challenged them to do this by regularly reading a small number of blogs which she searched for and selected. Although she asked her most advanced learner to make a judgement about the usefulness of the information contained in the blogs, her evaluation was based on the quality and range of language used by the authors. Here are two of the blogs she recommended:

- **Scobleizer:** http://scobleizer.com
  Written by Robert Scoble, formerly of Microsoft and a major player in the world of software development.

- **Musing of a Software Development Manager:** http://edgibbs.com
  The title says it all, although his thoughts are not limited to developing software.

Initially, she found that many of her learners said that they could not find the time to read these regularly or forgot to check the blog to see whether there were any new postings. Then one of the software engineers started to use an RSS reader to push the blog postings directly to his computer every day. Samantha began to do the same. She also started to produce simple exercises based on the latest postings. These began as vocabulary exercises using words and phrases from the blog. Later, she copied and pasted entire postings into a word-processor document and used them to create gap-fill exercises. For many of her learners, this proved to be a good motivation to keep track of what the bloggers were writing about. Even if they had not read the posting Samantha had used, they often looked at it afterwards

As the course progressed, it was agreed to drop some of the blogs which did not offer useful information or were not updated often enough. However, a few other blogs were added as the learners found the activity more and more useful and suggested new blogs they had found or been recommended. Eventually, the number of blogs being used stabilized at four, with the two listed above providing the majority of material for lessons.

Case study 2:
Using podcasts for authentic listening in the classroom

Kelly uses podcasts in the classroom with her intermediate group. She has two favourites:

- **The BBC's *From Our Own Correspondent* programme:**
  http://news.bbc.co.uk/1/hi/programmes/from_our_own_correspondent
  This has a number of short essays by BBC reporters from around the world; Kelly can access and print the transcripts of many of the reports from the same website.

- **The *Guardian Unlimited* podcasts:** http://www.guardian.co.uk/podcasts
  These consist of discussion programmes about science, arts and entertainment and a daily digest of the lead news stories.

Once she has downloaded the podcasts on to her own computer, Kelly listens to and selects one or two stories that she thinks will be of interest to her group and could provide them with useful vocabulary input. She makes a note of the counter times on her media player of exactly when these stories start and finish so that she can access them quickly in class. With the BBC programme, she prepares the transcript, and with the *Guardian* discussions, she finds a corresponding article from another part of the newspaper's website.

When she first started using podcasts, Kelly tried playing them using a computer in the classroom. Unfortunately, the sound quality through the computer's tiny on-board speaker was poor, and many of the class complained that they could not hear well enough. She now owns an iPod and a set of external speakers which plug into the iPod's headphone socket. She uses this set-up in class to play the podcast to her learners.

She varies her use of the podcasts. Sometimes the target is gist listening and the activity is the lead-in to a discussion about the topic. Sometimes she prepares more detailed questions and allows her learners to listen several times to catch the answers.

Some of her learners have started to download and listen to the podcasts before their classes with Kelly in order to be better prepared.

See page 140 for a lesson preparation sheet for this activity.

A wide range of electronic language-teaching materials are available to the contemporary teacher. Materials for the classroom can be downloaded from the Web and carried into the classroom in a traditional manner. Others can be used online, relying on the learner having access to a computer with an Internet connection. Yet others can be accessed from CD-ROMs. Some materials come with the recognizable stamp of established publishers. Meanwhile, others are from young language-teaching companies making use of the Web to reach a wider market or from individuals who are using the Web to share their ideas. This range of electronic material available to today's language teacher is frequently referred to as *blended learning.*

In this chapter, we will look at the three main formats for delivering electronic ELT materials before describing the types of material available and how you can access them. We will look at the many uses of such materials in ELT courses and also consider how the traditional language coursebook has been extended and supplemented by the inclusion of electronic components. The chapter will look at the Macmillan English Campus, which takes this trend one step further by placing a significant volume of a learner's course material onto the Web for access within and outside the classroom. Finally, we will take a look at some authoring tools which allow you to create interactive online materials for your own learners and anyone else who finds them useful.

Electronic formats

Electronic material for ELT can be divided into three basic formats: downloadable materials, online activities and materials on disks.

Downloadable materials

In the case of downloadable materials, once you have saved the files on your computer, your link to the Internet can be disconnected. Material intended to be printed, such as worksheets, or material which can be stored and distributed by email, such as mp3 files, are normally delivered by this method.

The most common computer file format for these kinds of materials is the pdf. In order to download a pdf file, you need to have Adobe Acrobat Reader installed on your computer. To check whether this is the case, click on the Start button and look for Adobe Reader in the programs list (or look in the Applications folder on a Mac). This program is often pre-installed on new computers and can also be found on the installation CD-ROMs from software companies. If you do not have it on your computer, you can download the latest version from http://www.adobe.com/products/acrobat/readstep2.html.

Once the reader program is on your computer, it runs automatically when you click on a link to download a pdf file. The reader program opens inside your browser. The time required for the download depends on the number of pages in the pdf. The reader program has its own tool bar, which includes a save button and a print button. Use these to save a copy of the pdf on your computer's hard drive and to produce a hard copy, respectively.

Online materials

In contrast to downloadable materials, these rely on the learners having access to a computer connected to the Internet. Online exercises, tests, games and listening activities often require little programs that integrate with your browser. These are known as *plug-ins*. There are a small number of plug-ins which are widely used and, therefore, essential to any web user who wants to do more than read text or view images.

Audio/video plug-ins

There are three programs which are most commonly used to hear audio and view video. It is useful to have all three installed, since the audio and video files they can play are not always mutually compatible. Each is available to download from the URLs below.

- Windows Media Player
  http://www.microsoft.com/windows/windowsmedia
- RealPlayer
  http://www.real.com
- QuickTime
  http://www.apple.com/quicktime

Animation/interaction plug-ins

There are two further plug-ins that are almost universally used for animation and interaction. These are the Flash and Shockwave players. If you click on a link that requires these plug-ins and they are not installed on your computer, then you are given the option to automatically download and install them. Both can be downloaded from http://www.macromedia.com/downloads.

Material on disk

Finally, some materials are available in disk format. A CD-ROM is essentially a storage device. It can store digital data in formats such as text, pictures, photographs, animations, video clips and audio clips. CD-ROMs offer language learners the exciting possibilities of a multimedia environment, allowing them to move between the various media at will. There are also DVDs, the main difference being that these offer a lot more storage space.

Loading CD-ROMs has never been easier. Many computers are set up with an auto-run function, which means that you just insert them into the disk drive, and they install automatically. If not, you need to click on My computer and then click on a file, which is usually called 'set up.exe'. When you install a CD-ROM, you may need to follow the on-screen instructions, and perhaps make some choices about which type of installation you prefer – full or customized. Some disks need to use certain programs, such as Apple QuickTime or a new version of Flash, and you are often asked if you would like to install them. Network versions of some CD-ROMs may be of interest to self-access managers.

Types and sources of ELT materials

The Internet has changed both the format and distribution of material, and has become in itself a rich and almost infinite source of ELT materials. These are not only provided by publishers, but also by practising language teachers. The range of materials provided is extremely broad, and to attempt an exhaustive survey is beyond the scope of this book. However, the examples and sources below will give you a flavour of what is available.

Worksheets and other materials

Worksheets and other materials are available for classroom use, homework or self-study. You can find specific materials for young learners, Business English and special purposes, exam preparation, skills work and ESOL. You can also access lessons written by other working teachers and get ideas and tips for use in the classroom. In most cases, you will use a computer only to find and download the materials from the Web and then print them.

The main UK ELT publishers each have websites offering a range of materials to download. These have often been written by established authors and cover the whole range of different language-learning situations.

- Cambridge University Press
  http://www.cambridge.org/elt
- Longman
  http://www.longman.com
- Macmillan – OneStopEnglish
  http://www.onestopenglish.com
- Oxford University Press
  http://www.oup.com/elt

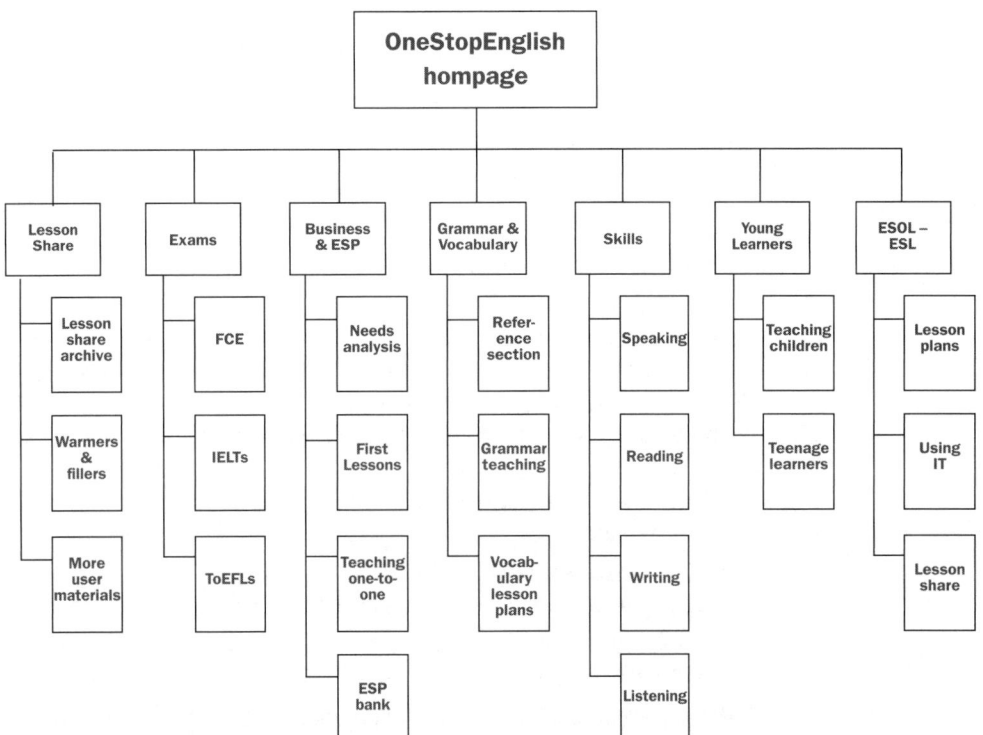

Figure 3.1
Some of the sections on the OneStopEnglish website

As well as publishers' websites, there are many other websites offering downloadable materials and lesson ideas. These are often provided by teachers from around the world who have used these websites and want to share their ideas. Amongst the most popular are:

- Dave Sperling's ESL Café
  http://www.eslcafe.com
- English Club
  http://www.englishclub.com
- eslbase
  http://www.eslbase.com

Exercises and tests

Many exercises available online and on CD-ROM focus on grammar and vocabulary. Such exercises are an ideal way to practise discrete items such as contrasting two structures (eg *since* and *for*) or confusable words (eg *continuous* vs *continual*). Among the most common activity types are multiple choice, in which the user has to select the correct answer from a number of choices, possibly displayed in a drop-down menu; gap-fill, typing in the answer using the keyboard; and drag and drop, where the user clicks on an item and pulls it to the correct position within a text or matches it with another item on the screen.

This interactive medium is perfect for creating exercises which replicate those formats typically used in ELT tests and examinations: true/false, multiple choice and so on. Exam-practice disks on CD-ROM are very popular, as learners can do unlimited extra practice. CD-ROMs have also been used to deliver adaptive tests, such as OUP's Quick Placement Test. These adapt the sequence of questions depending on how successful the learner is in order to better assess the learner's level.

Interactive online materials can be found on publishers' and independent websites. Some examples can be found at:

- EFLnet
  http://www.eflnet.com
- OUP Test It, Fix It test
  http://www.oup.com/elt/global/products/testitfixit/test

Vocabulary reference

Vocabulary input for learners includes specialist vocabulary for ESP areas. Business English is well served on the Web. Learners can access functional language for situations such as making telephone calls or giving presentations. There are also websites which offer colloquial language, jargon and idiomatic expressions, all of which can be used to enrich the language of high-level learners. Each of the following sites provides links to categorized vocabulary lists.

- About.com English Vocabulary
  http://esl.about.com/od/engilshvocabulary
- BBC Learning English
  http://www.bbc.co.uk/worldservice/learningenglish
- Dictionary of English Idioms
  http://www.usingenglish.com/reference/idioms

CD-ROMs can be particularly useful for vocabulary, since they often include a searchable glossary of key words included on the disk.

Language games

Games are another electronic alternative to books and paper-based exercises. They are principally aimed at younger learners, although there are also games which can be used by adults. They focus on topics such as vocabulary, spelling and grammar.

Arcade-style games require the learner to use the mouse or cursor keys on the keyboard to move elements around the screen or click on the correct item. They often have sound effects and music, as well as a time limit and a score to show the learner's success rate. Other games, such as quizzes, crosswords and hangman, also have scores and timers, but they are often less frenetic and therefore may appeal to older learners. The following websites are sources of games for use online:

- British Council Learn English Central
  http://www.britishcouncil.org/learnenglish-central-games-homepage.htm
  The British Council offers a large number of games which cover many areas of language. These range from single-screen drag-and-drop exercises which practise specialist vocabulary to the extensive Agents Underground, which requires players to solve puzzles in a tour of the London Underground and emails new passwords for entry to each new part of the game.
- English Word Games
  http://www.learn-english-today.com/wordgames.html
- Free English Games
  http://www.free-english-games.com
- Interesting Things for ESL Learners
  http://www.manythings.org

Language games on CD-ROM can be more sophisticated again. The latest games include large-scale and challenging simulations, which involve making complex decisions. Some of the most inventive disks are those created for children and young adults, involving excellent animations, and activities devised to provide fun and enjoyment.

Listening activities

Listening activities are available through all three electronic formats described above.

There are two types of listening activities available as podcasts: those produced by staff at academic institutions or commercial language-course providers, and those by enthusiastic teachers around the world. The style of these recordings varies from closely scripted examples of spoken English designed to focus on specific grammatical, lexical or functional content to more relaxed, entertaining monologues or dialogues intended to provide examples of 'real' English in a context. These podcasts are usually accompanied by support material such as a transcript or vocabulary list. The following websites can be useful sources of podcasts for your classroom.

- ESLpod
  http://www.eslpod.com
- TOEFL Podcast
  http://www.eslpod.com/toefl
- EnglishFeed
  http://englishfeed.com
- The Language Key – Business English Pod
  http://lkey.podomatic.com

To search for other ESL/EFL podcasts, visit Englishcaster, a directory website dedicated to listing these types of website: http://www.englishcaster.com.

Online listening activities are divided into those that are specifically scripted for English learners, while others consist of authentic materials which have been specially selected. The BBC World Service's Learning English website (http://www.bbc.co.uk/worldservice/learningenglish) offers both types of activity (see Figure 3.2). For example:

- News English
  A short report from the BBC World Service international radio news with a short summary, transcript and a glossary of some vocabulary items.
- Watch and Listen

Specially recorded five-minute audio reports and transcripts on subjects such as famous people, entertainment and pop music.

Figure 3.2
BBC Learning
English website

Sections of the BBC Learning English website that contain listening activities

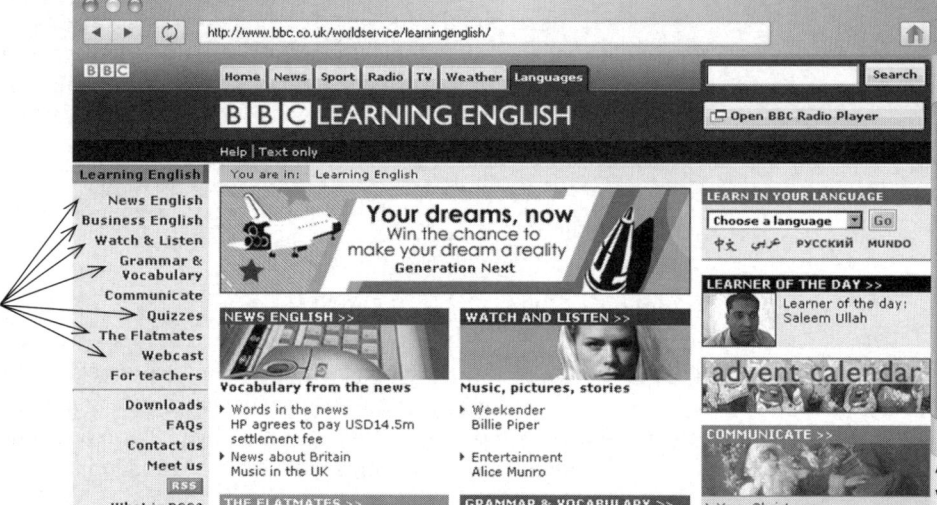

Finally, many CD-ROMs contain audio and video clips. Learners can listen to audio clips as many times as they like, gaining exposure to short phrases or more extensive listenings, with the possibility of pausing at will and listening again to specific sections of the clip. In the case of video, learners can choose whether to watch a video clip with or without subtitles. They can also often view a transcript which contains hyperlinks to translations or definitions of certain words.

Reading, speaking, writing and pronunciation

Interactive materials on the Web and on CD-ROM offer opportunities to develop language skills, such as reading, speaking, writing and pronunciation. While reading a text on-screen, learners can click on a word and bring up an explanation in a new window. This type of access to meaning on demand can be useful for learners. They can print off longer articles and read them off-screen.

Fluency practice is usually organized by the teacher, and is an area which is less catered for by electronic ELT material. However, some limited speaking practice is available on CD-ROM. Learners can read and record alternate lines in a dialogue, and then play back the complete dialogue. Generally, learners are asked to evaluate their own utterances, and they also have the chance to keep on practising and refining their attempts in order to improve. There are opportunities for freer speaking away from the computer. Learners can discuss in pairs their answers to an on-screen exercise, for instance.

CD-ROMs are an excellent medium for providing guided writing practice, although opportunities for free composition are limited. Some writing CD-ROMs have an email facility so that the final product of a writing task can be emailed to the teacher for evaluation and marking.

CD-ROMs can also be helpful in the area of pronunciation. On some disks, the learner can click on a version of the phonemic chart and listen to the individual phonemes. Some disks display the intonation pattern the learner uses in visual format. Speech-recognition technology can indicate to learners whether they are approximating a sound by giving positive or negative feedback. For more ideas on using CD-ROMs for pronunciation work, see Chapter 4.

Combining technology and coursebook support

Nowadays, the coursebook is just one component in a suite of material, which may include both CD-ROMs and online exercises. Selecting the best mix of materials for a course is nowadays an increasingly important part of the teacher's role. Recently, the range and variety of support material offered by publishing companies has grown tremendously. One particular product, the Macmillan English Campus, offers exciting ways of integrating online material into courses, as a complement to paper-based material or an alternative. Enterprising teachers can also create their own interactive materials.

This mix of media to support a taught language course is often considered as one example of blended learning. In a blended-learning model, the teacher in the face-to-face course component offers in-class explanations of tricky areas in response to learner questions. The teacher is there to personalize the practice of grammatical structures and explore unlikely examples. The learner is supported by a range of paper-based materials, such as a workbook of practice exercises and a grammar reference book, as well as electronic support material.

CD-ROM coursebook support

A recent trend has been to include a CD-ROM or multi-ROM in the back of the coursebook. The latter can be used both as an ordinary audio CD and with a computer as an interactive CD-ROM. You issue the coursebook and ask learners to load the disk on their own PC. This enables the learner to follow the course unit by unit, doing extra grammar activities, listening or pronunciation work on CD-ROM. Some disks allow learners to select the exercises they wish to revisit and create a customized sequence of activities, saving the results of the exercises they do. Learners can also record the vocabulary they find useful in a personalized vocabulary notebook.

Online coursebook support

The support offered by publishers' websites can be rich and varied. As you work through a coursebook, you can get extra ideas for your lesson. This unit-by-unit support may consist of hyperlinks to websites which extend the content of each chapter. A bilingual glossary with vocabulary translations may be exactly what you need for a monolingual group working in a particular country. There is a wealth of more general support, such as free lesson plans, online grammar and vocabulary exercises and webquests. Some additional resources are available which schools and private individuals can sign up for and pay for online. Some sites include author interviews and forums for users of the coursebook around the world.

In addition to interactive exercises online, you can access e-lessons. An *e-lesson* is a term used by Macmillan for an off-the-shelf worksheet which offers a free-standing classroom activity. The worksheet is downloadable and delivered across the globe via the Web as a pdf. Simply click on the link on the e-lesson web page, print the pdf as many times as necessary, or print one and photocopy it for everyone in the group. It is accompanied by a set of teacher's notes. To subscribe to an e-lesson, go to Inside Out (http://www.insideout.net).

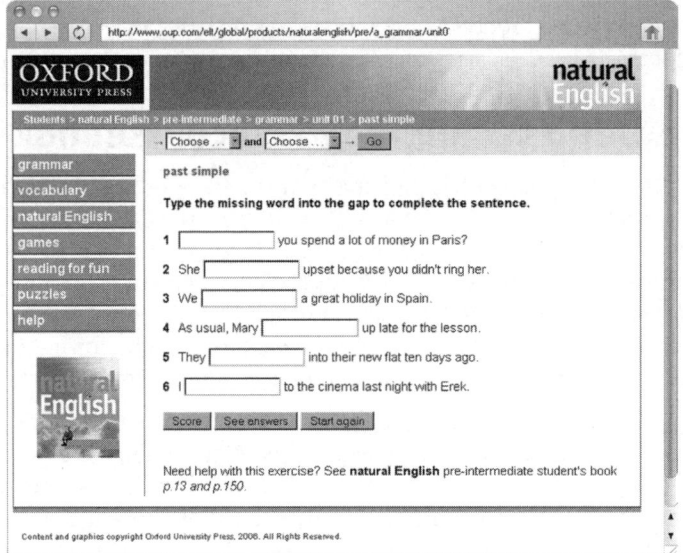

Figure 3.3
Interactive exercise to
support a coursebook
unit: you can send the
learners to the site
during the lesson to
do further practice on
the simple past

© Oxford University Press www.oup.com/elt/naturalenglish

Supporting a course with the Macmillan English Campus (MEC)

Some language schools wishing to add a technology strand to their taught courses may consider buying a suite of ready-made, online materials and then customizing them with the school's own logo. This is often financially more attractive than embarking on a material-creation project.

One unique option which is proving attractive to chain schools and universities across the world is the Macmillan English Campus. This was first developed in 2003 as part of a blended-learning solution, so that classroom teaching is complemented and supported by online learning.

The Macmillan English Campus is an Internet-based, interactive learning environment that helps learners to practise English. It contains a database of over 2,500 interactive activities, covering grammar, vocabulary, listening and pronunciation practice. It also contains news articles, tests, webquests, language games, grammar reference units and preparation exercises for the Cambridge ESOL and TOEFL exams. The Campus comprises material for adult, general English and Business English courses. The material covers six language levels, from beginner to advanced.

An organization wishing to buy into the Macmillan English Campus pays for a number of user IDs. You start the course by issuing all the learners in the class with a password to the Campus. The English Campus can be used both inside and outside the language classroom. It can be integrated into a class, for vocabulary development, grammar work and skills work. When you use the Campus during the lesson, you can show it through an electronic projector or interactive whiteboard, or by having learners go online if computers are available. If these options are not possible, you can book a lesson in the school's self-access centre.

The learner can also access the Campus at home. It can be used outside class in a structured way, for homework, and for consolidating and reviewing language. It can also be used in a less structured way, with learners choosing to do extra activities such as playing language games, or reading and listening for pleasure. Learners can store their new vocabulary in an electronic notebook, which they can use to review at home.

One interesting feature of the Campus is that texts are posted to the users each week at three different language levels (elementary, intermediate and advanced). This enables learners to study up-to-date material. These texts are adapted from the *Guardian Weekly*. They are topical, with a mid-term shelf life. At the bottom of the article is a series of follow-up questions ('Food for thought') which you can activate in class. A practical activity at the end of this chapter looks at ways in which these texts can be exploited.

There are a number of ways that the Campus can be integrated into a course. MEC can be accessed using three profiles: learner, teacher and administrator. Access as an administrator enables the use of sophisticated course-building tools in order to create a syllabus for a particular group of learners. Course-building tools allow institutions to pick resources and activities from the database to suit specific class needs. A course can be created without a link to published materials – an attractive option for certain courses where learners are not following a particular coursebook. Alternatively, a school can use one of the pre-prepared courses created in Campus. These courses can be altered at any time, and exercises and units of study can be added or removed. In all, the Campus provides a flexible online material bank which can be used to complement a coursebook or on a program which is not using a coursebook.

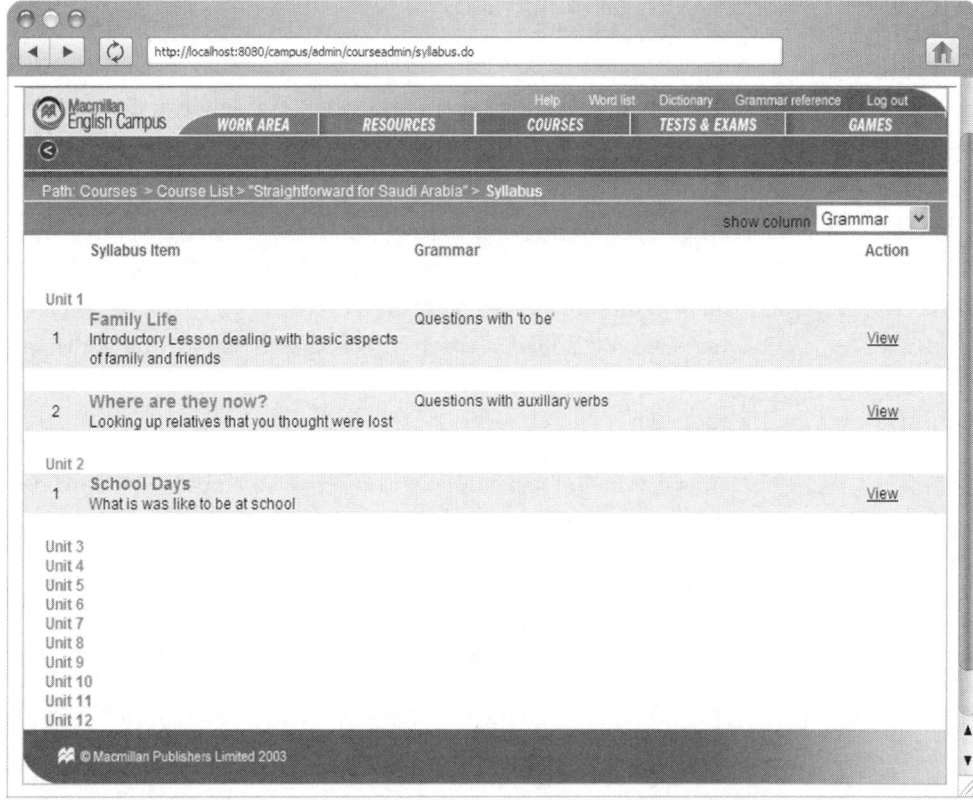

Figure 3.4 Course-creation tool: building a course using the syllabus of Straightforward *(Macmillan)*

Creating your own online materials

A final option is to create your own materials that fit your learners' needs exactly. If you have your own website or are able to place pages on the website of the institute where you teach, you have the opportunity to create interactive exercises for your learners to access and use. The easiest way to do this is to use authoring software.

A popular piece of software for authoring exercises is Hot Potatoes, which is free to anyone who works in a non-profit-making educational institution or context and is prepared to post the exercises they create on a website which is accessible to anyone using the Web. Hot Potatoes enables you to create the following types of exercises:

- multiple-choice quizzes
- gap-fill texts
- ordering and matching activities
- jumbled sentences and words
- crosswords.

To download the installation files, register and access tutorials on using Hot Potatoes, go to Half-Baked Software Inc's website: http://web.uvic.ca/hrd/hotpot/index.htm.

There are lots of existing examples of exercises which you can view to get an idea of what is possible with the software. Here are two web pages which provide links to some of the best examples on the Web:

- Half-Baked Software Inc
  http://web.uvic.ca/hrd/hotpot/sites6.htm
  The websites on this list are not exclusively aimed at English-language learning, but do demonstrate the range of exercises that can be created with the Hot Potatoes programs.

- English Online
  http://cla.univ-fcomte.fr/english/html/hotpot.htm
  A list of 'technically interesting' Hot Potatoes web pages which show how far the output of the software can be modified.

Other authoring software which can be used to create interactive language exercises include:

- Quandary
  http://www.halfbakedsoftware.com/quandary.php
  This is from the same people who wrote Hot Potatoes. It can be used to create maze exercises, in which learners are given options and have to make choices in order to progress.

- MaxAuthor
  http://cali.arizona.edu/docs/wmaxa
  An authoring tool that allows you to integrate audio with texts to create language exercises.

Opportunities and issues

There are many opportunities and benefits afforded by creating the right mix of electronic materials, online and offline, to enrich a language course.

Appropriacy and reliability

The Web can be used as a virtual resource bank and library. There are purpose-made materials for topics, grammar points, vocabulary development, and skills development. However, there is so much material that the first consideration is locating the best places to find what you want. When you have found material, you need to evaluate it quickly in terms of how useful it is to you and work out how to use it with minimum preparation and maximum impact.

An important skill for you to develop is the ability to evaluate the materials you are using, either downloaded from the Web or for use online. The golden rule for these materials is to try them out yourself beforehand, to see what problems, if any, your learners may encounter. Your assessment will also include whether the level is right, the suitability for the age of your learners, and the appropriacy and usefulness of the language covered. You may also need to take into account cultural issues. Ask yourself whether the subject matter of the material will cause embarrassment to your learners. It is also useful to reflect on the outcome of the lesson and decide how successful it was, both in terms of the lesson as a whole and the integration of the new material. Did you encounter any problems? What would you change next time?

For a useful list of specific evaluation criteria for use with materials taken from the Web, see page 141.

Given the range available, narrowing your search to reliable sources is important. The main benefit of using material from established publishers is the knowledge that it has been written and edited to a high standard. Such material is often accompanied by detailed teacher's notes, which makes it very useful for less experienced teachers. Materials from websites with a less professional provenance need to be treated with more caution.

Motivation

One of the greatest possibilities of electronic ELT materials is the increase in motivation some learners experience.

An attraction of online and CD-ROM coursebook support is that it offers variety, and a change from working through the 'same old exercise in the same old coursebook'.

A lot of electronic ELT materials have similar content to exercises or tests in books and appeal to learners who find using a mouse and keyboard more motivating than writing. They also provide instant feedback.

Games especially appeal to younger learners as an alternative to traditional classroom-style teaching. Many young and teenage learners enjoy games for their own sake, but this is not always the case with adults. If you want your learners to play games, you should explain why and what benefit you believe they will derive from it. Even with younger learners, tell them why they are playing the game and afterwards test them on the language that was covered by it.

A further motivating factor is that learners may feel empowered: they can work through the material at their own speed. For example, learners decide how many times they wish to listen to an audio clip and how many attempts they wish to make at an exercise. They can choose their own pathway through the material, so they may choose whether to work systematically in a linear way or take advantage of the non-linear aspect of a CD-ROM, for example.

Enhanced listening

Listening using podcasts, online audio or CD-ROM can be integrated into any part of a language course, provided the facilities are available. You can use online listening in the classroom; your learners can listen individually through headphones in a self-access centre; and they can listen at home or in the office as self-study or homework.

Although the Web is awash with audio clips, live streamed audio and video, and podcasts, much of this authentic material is unsuitable for language learners. It is too fast, contains too much idiomatic language, and has unfamiliar accents. Specially produced listening material avoids many of these problems. However, as with the other types of material discussed above, it is important to make your own assessment about the quality and usefulness of the material you offer your learners.

The advantage offered by podcasts is that they can be used in the classroom via a computer with speakers or by linking a digital music player to speakers. Alternatively, your learners can download them to their own music players to listen to outside the class. On the whole, the podcasts provided by the sites listed in this chapter are aimed at self-study, but they can all be easily adapted for use in the classroom.

Up-to-date content

The ease with which websites can be updated means that material online can be more up to date than that provided through print. By providing materials via the Internet, a publisher can ensure that the coursebook is kept up to date. Similarly, one of the most important benefits of vocabulary websites is often their currency. This is especially the case with slang or jargon.

E-lessons, too, are usually topical, and may provide exactly the right material for you at just the right moment. They could provide material for something in the news or for a regular event, such as Christmas or Valentine's day. For example, in Business English, the coursebook may include a text on the Enron scandal. This text can be updated through using an e-lesson which refers to a current event. The text of the e-lesson may begin as follows: 'Many felt justice had been done when two former bosses of Enron were found guilty last month. (2006)'. After the lesson, learners can go to the Internet to research information on more recent developments.

Flexibility

Much electronic material can be used flexibly in terms of level, and should be viewed as a multi-level resource. Even though a CD-ROM, for example, has been designed for learners in a particular level band (beginner, elementary, intermediate or advanced), a learner can use a disk which is lower than their official level in order to consolidate language. Equally, they can select material at a higher level in order to challenge themselves.

Another way in which electronic material can be used flexibly is the way in which it can be combined with paper-based materials in order to meet the language needs of a particular group of learners. As seen earlier, electronic material such as the Macmillan English Campus allows you to customize courses using both online and paper-based material, to suit the group's requirements. Another approach involves integrating web-based activities (such as webquests) with published coursebooks and creating supplementary materials designed to promote communication and collaboration. This has been described as a *blended-book solution*. For examples of this approach, see http://www.24hours.it/wq/E-biz.doc.

Some CD-ROMs offer authoring opportunities. These are largely underused, in our experience, as teachers are already busy enough managing the course content. However, the chance to customize language games by inputting your own examples may be useful.

Finally, creating your own interactive materials presents further opportunities. You have complete control over the language content of the exercises. This includes not only the language being tested or presented in the exercises, but also the rubric. You can create exercises that fit closely with the course you are teaching. The ease with which exercises can be created means that you can use lists of vocabulary or feedback on learner mistakes that result from a lesson and turn them into exercises in a very short time.

Practical activities

Finding and using ESP materials

Aim: to find and use materials for the language of contract law

Level: upper intermediate to advanced

Interaction: one-to-one

Technology: downloadable worksheet and teacher's notes

Rationale: This is an example of how to find appropriate materials from a publisher's website. In this situation, you require material which covers a specialized area important for the learner, who could be a lawyer or senior sales manager. You may or may not have any expertise in this area, but are relying on the fact that the worksheet is on the website of an established publisher of language-training material.

Before class:

1 Visit the OneStopEnglish website at http://www.onestopenglish.com.

2 Click on the following links: Business and ESP > Business ESP Bank > ESP Bank: Legal > ESP Bank: Legal – The law of Contract.

3 At the bottom of this web page is a box labelled Related Pages. Click on the link for the worksheet and the teacher's notes. Each will open in a separate browser window using the Acrobat Reader plug-in.

4 Print a copy of the teacher's notes for yourself and two copies of the worksheet for you and your learner. Spend a little time before the lesson doing the exercise yourself and checking the answers with the teacher's notes.

Procedure:

1 Introduce the topic and give your learner the worksheet.

2 Work through each page of the worksheet with the learner. Make use of either a general or specialist legal language dictionary to check words if necessary.

3 The final stage on the worksheet consists of a number of discussion topics. If there is time in the lesson, ask your learner his or her opinion about each of these. Alternatively, ask the learner to select one of the topics and to prepare a short presentation about it for the next lesson.

Follow on: As with much ESP, you do not need to be an expert in this area. If any legal questions do come up, suggest that the learner takes the responsibility to research the answer, either using the Web or by contacting a colleague, and be ready to provide an answer by the next lesson.

Conditional conundrum

Aim: to raise awareness of the conditional structure

Level: upper intermediate and higher

Interaction: group work and feedback

Technology: CD-ROM and Internet

Rationale: Learners need to be made aware of both standard constructions and non-standard forms. The latter may include less frequent language, such as *If we would have … and If I've done it by then*, and unfinished conditionals such as *I'd never've done that*. The Internet is a repository of such non-standard language; grammar reference material tends to showcase standard forms. This exercise promotes noticing and a process grammar approach as described by Thornbury in *Uncovering Grammar* (2001).

Before class: Bring in a few grammar reference books. Check Internet access is available, and that learners can access a grammar reference CD-ROM.

Procedure:

1 Ask learners to tell you how many conditional forms there are in English. Write their answers on the whiteboard. A typical group will produce answers ranging from three to six plus.

2 Divide the group into research teams. Tell them to check their assumptions using the following tools:

Group 1: a grammar reference book, such as *Oxford Practice Grammar Advanced* (OUP).

Group 2: a grammar CD-ROM, or the unit on conditionals in the courseware.

Group 3: the Web. This group should create examples of conditional sentences in order to type them into a search engine such as Google.

Groups re-form to include one person from each research team. The learners discuss their findings.

3 The learners report back on any differences in the information provided by the various source materials, and any amendments they would like to make to their original figures (Step 1).

4 Debrief the task. What have they learned about the conditional form? Which source do they find most reliable/complete?

Variations: This research activity can be used with other areas of grammar, such as the use of articles and the number of modal verbs in English.

Exploiting the headline news

Acknowledgement for the original idea: Christiane Khatchadourian / Reinaldo Campos

Aim: to predict the content of a text; to exploit the fact that learners have access to an authentic text customized to different levels; to work on vocabulary-storing techniques

Level: elementary and above, depending on the choice of text

Interaction: groupwork / individual work

Technology: Macmillan English Campus (MEC). For those teaching without the MEC, a variation of this activity can be done using a text at three different levels from OneStopEnglish; certain CD-ROMs offer the possibility of storing vocabulary in an electronic workbook

Rationale: MEC provides a weekly news article for extra reading practice; it is available in three bands of language ability. There are benefits from exploiting the fact that the learners have access to an article which has been simplified to three different levels. For example, they can study an easier level of a text in class, and then read the higher-level version at home, having been sensitized to the language already. The Campus includes access to the MED online and provides an electronic vocabulary notebook. Both of these features can be used in-class. Familiarizing the learners with these tools may well encourage them to use the tools outside the classroom for self-study, and thereby promote learner autonomy.

Before class: You need to check the three titles of the latest article. Transfer the titles onto an OHT, with the most difficult (and shortest) title first, and the easiest (and longest) title last. If you are not using the MEC in the lesson, you will need to print off hard copies of the article at the appropriate level.

Procedure:

1 Use the titles of the articles as a prediction exercise for the text. Reveal the titles in sequence, pausing between titles to elicit ideas about what the text is about, eg
Audrey heads a quiet revolution
Audrey look heads a change in women's attitudes
The Audrey Hepburn look starts a change in women's attitudes

2 Exploit the article in class as you would for a normal reading lesson. For example, reading for gist, work on vocabulary, etc. Use the 'Food for thought' discussion questions at the foot of the text.

3 To finish, the learners can add new words into their electronic notebooks. Encourage learners to organize their new words into categories, and create their own personalized example sentences.

Follow up: If you have used the level 2 text in class, then challenge the learners by suggesting they read the level 3 text at home.

Variations: The learners can read the 'easy' level first in order to get a summary of the text; then they read the 'average' or 'difficult' level, with the MED online open.

Case studies

Case study 1:
Creating customized online materials

Lisa teaches English at a university. The university has a website and a system that allows all teaching staff to add web pages with information for their learners. The university uses Hot Potatoes, and its e-learning support department provides short training courses for lecturers and teachers who wish to use it to make exercises for their section of the website. Lisa attended one of these courses and decided to create some exercises for her summer classes.

She had quickly discovered that her learners enjoyed using computer exercises to learn vocabulary or to consolidate their grammatical knowledge. However, the exercises available on the Web or on CD-ROMs never fitted closely enough with the classes she was preparing and teaching. She wanted to have greater control over the lexis used in the exercises and to have a closer correlation between the structures covered during class time and the material the learners used in self-study.

She used a feature of Hot Potatoes called JMatch to make drag-and-drop vocabulary exercises in which learners had to match verbs with nouns to make collocations they had seen in class. She also used a feature called JMix to create jumbled sentences which demonstrated the grammatical structures which the learners were reviewing. As the course progressed, she also used JQuiz to create a set of multiple-choice questions to go with texts that she wanted her learners to study. The questions focused on the structure, style and punctuation of the text.

Initially, Lisa found that it took a long time to create each exercise. Despite the training course, she relied on trial and error and eventually identified the way of working that suited her. The most important thing she realized early on was not to start building an exercise until she had written all the content. Once she established this rule for herself, the work of using Hot Potatoes to make an exercise became very fast, and the quality of the exercises also improved, since she could spend more time on writing the content.

Once the first set of exercises was complete, she placed them on the university website using tools which the e-learning support department had installed on her computer. During the summer, she created a whole set of exercises which integrated with the course.

At the end of each lesson with her class, she gave them the web address of the exercise and set it as homework to be completed before the next lesson. When that lesson arrived, she followed up with a review of the content of the exercise, then set a writing task for homework that required the learners to put into practice the issues covered. Her learners quickly adapted to this way of working and only failed to complete the homework on a few isolated occasions due to problems with individual's computers.

Since all the exercises were stored on the university website, she was able to reuse them on subsequent courses, and they were available for her colleagues to use or adapt for their own courses.

Case study 2:
Using a presentations CD-ROM

John, a Business English teacher, decided to run a presentations course following a blended-learning model, so half the course was run in face-to-face sessions and the rest of the course involved learners working at home. The self-study component incorporated a CD-ROM. In the first lesson, he met his group and brainstormed ten tips for giving an effective presentation. He discussed with the group the topics of their final presentation and issued the learners with the CD-ROM *Effective Presentations* (York Associates). John told the learners that the language of presentations comprises many fixed phrases, such as *I've divided my presentation into three parts*, etc. He pointed out that many learners say *I am divide my presentation into three parts*. By using the CD-ROM, learners could practise these phrases at the computer. The learners' homework consisted of watching videos of good presenters, and doing guided speaking practice at home. In class, John offered learners the chance to do a dry run. In the last face-to-face class, the learners stood up and delivered their presentation to the group, while John completed individual feedback sheets.

After the course, during the course feedback, John asked how they found the CD-ROM. Most of them used it. Some learners said they really appreciated the chance to watch different presenters' styles. All the learners agreed that the fact that they knew they had to deliver the final presentation in class had an effect on the way they prepared, and that they did more work as the deadline approached. Overall, John felt that the course worked effectively as a blended-learning course.

A wide range of electronic dictionaries is available to teachers and learners, and can be a useful addition to any course. Their capabilities allow the user to look up words quickly, and they have a wider range of functions than their print equivalents. They often have additional examples, too. This chapter will look at dictionaries on CD-ROMs and online, as well as e-dictionaries and pocket translators. This chapter will also look at another electronic resource which, while not strictly a dictionary, is a powerful electronic search tool: the concordancer.

CD-ROM dictionaries offer learners the chance to expand their vocabulary, both inside and outside the classroom. Incorporating the pronunciation opportunities of a CD-ROM dictionary is a good example of blended learning in action. The learners can work in the self-access centre or at home, using the technology to work on the pronunciation of a difficult sound, in preparation for giving a presentation to the teacher and the class.

How to use electronic dictionaries

CD-ROM dictionaries

A CD-ROM version of a dictionary is often included at the back of the paper-based version, and some of them are also available as stand-alone versions. However, it is not uncommon for learners and teachers to be unaware of the features and benefits of using a CD-ROM dictionary simply because they have never loaded the disk. It has never been easier to install the program, and nowadays this usually involves making a number of simple on-screen choices. For example, you may be asked if you would like a 'full' installation, which copies all the sound files to your hard drive, or a 'customised' installation, which takes less memory. The inlay card which comes with each CD-ROM provides any technical specifications, such as the system requirements. Most CD-ROMs come with a user guide with useful information about the features of the disk; also, there is usually a help file on the disk itself, or an interactive guided tour. Once you have loaded the disk, a shortcut icon will appear on your desktop which gives you quick and easy access to the dictionary.

Searching

One of the most important and popular features of CD-ROM dictionaries is the search function. Type the word you wish to look up in the search box, press the Enter key or a Find/Go button, and part or all of the dictionary entry will be displayed. As you enter each letter of a word, the dictionary shows all the words which start with this letter or combination of letters. This feature of a CD-ROM dictionary can be very helpful for learners who may not be sure about the exact spelling of a word. Dictionary CD-ROMs allow you to search using 'wildcards': the symbol ? represents a missing letter, whereas * indicates that there may be additional letters. Again, this feature can be useful in finding a word if you are not sure how to spell it, or if you wish to find derivatives in your search. Typing 'econom*' will produce a return that includes *economics, economist, economical* and *economically*. You can also search for all the words which start or end with a particular prefix or suffix. Typing 'auto*' into the search box will pull up a list of all the words beginning with *auto*.

CD-ROM dictionaries also include powerful advanced search features. These features make it possible to further refine a search, in the same way that it is possible to restrict a search when using an Internet search engine. On the *Macmillan English Dictionary*, for instance, you can restrict your search by various criteria, such as parts of speech, frequency, register or grammar. The user can search the dictionary for all the phrasal verbs which end with *up*, or all the words that have been labelled as 'business' or 'legal'.

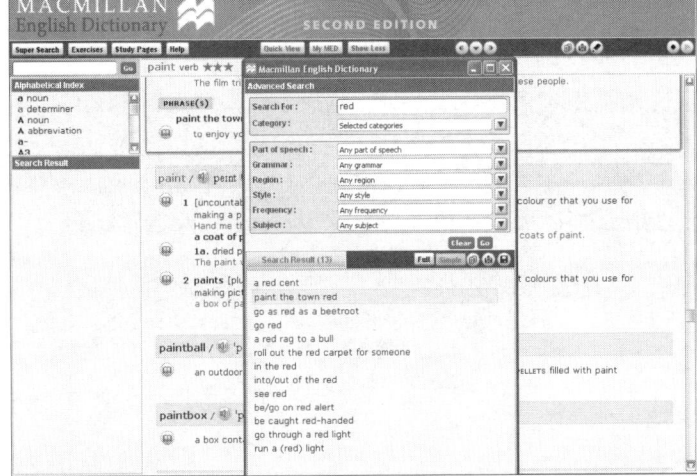

Figure 4.1
How to customize a search using the Advanced Search feature on the Macmillan English Dictionary for Advanced Learners

Pronunciation

An electronic dictionary can help learners in the area of pronunciation, and the inclusion of sound files and audio clips is an exciting key feature. Whereas print dictionaries only provide phonemic script, CD-ROM dictionaries offer learners the chance to listen to words. In a monolingual English learner's dictionary on CD-ROM, next to the entry for each word, there are usually two symbols, one to listen to the British English model and one to hear the word in American English. Learners can listen to a word in the variety of their choice as many times as they wish, just by clicking on the symbol. If they have a microphone, they can practise repeating a word and play it back, comparing their effort with the original. They can rerecord themselves, and so work towards improving their pronunciation of a word they find difficult. (See Figure 4.2.)

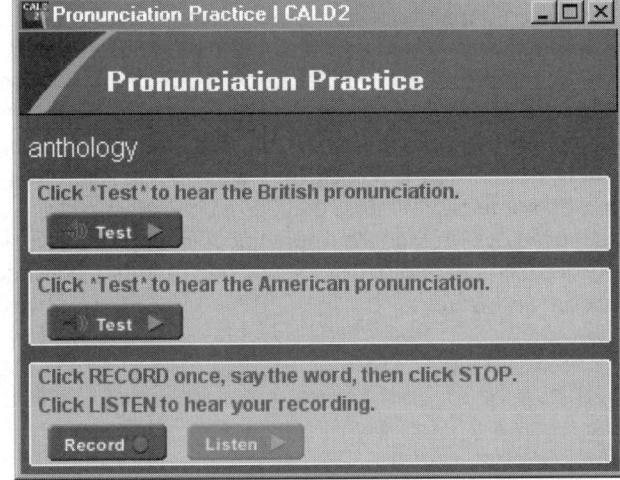

Figure 4.2
Pronunciation practice feature on the Cambridge Advanced Learner's Dictionary

Audio clips on CD-ROM include some words which may be more easily described by a sound than a definition, such as *flush, cough* and *sneeze.*

The *Macmillan English Dictionary (MED)* also includes a Sound Search function, which enables learners to perform searches using the phonemic symbols. This enables users to look up words that they may have heard but never seen written down; one example would be /trɒf/. It also allows you to compile lists of words that may sound similar but are spelled differently (see Figure 4.3).

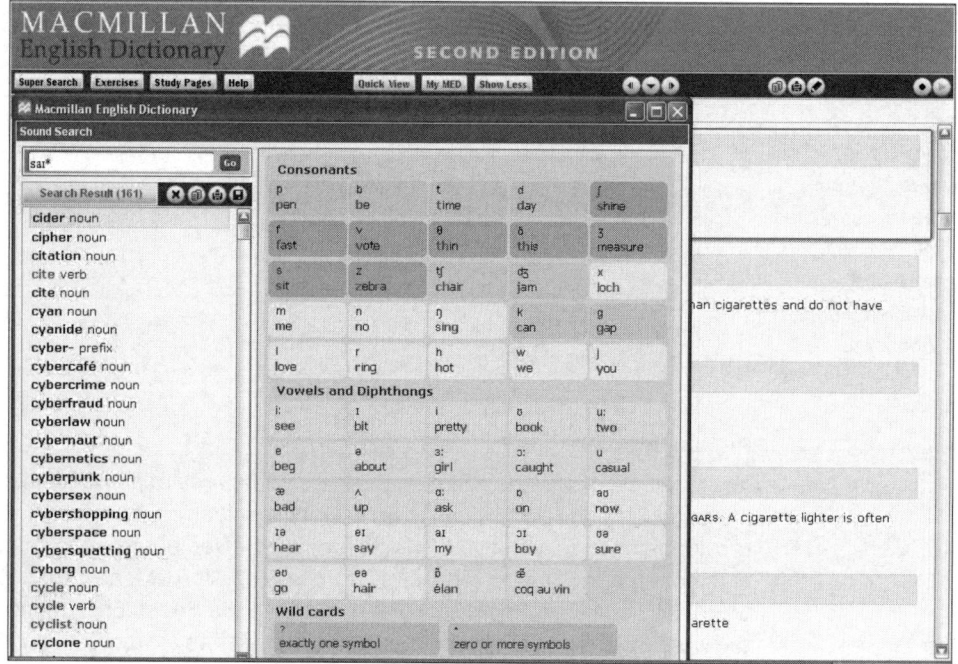

Figure 4.3 Sound Search function on the Macmillan English Dictionary. *The user has searched for all words beginning with* /saɪ/.

Using a CD-ROM dictionary with a web page

A key advantage of electronic dictionaries is that definitions are available more immediately than in print equivalents. It is possible to minimize the CD-ROM display, so that the user has the dictionary in a small 'window', which he or she can move around the computer screen at will. When looking at a web page, a learner can be running the dictionary at the same time. As the user moves the cursor over a word on the web page, the definition appears instantly in this window – providing it is in the dictionary, of course. In a number of electronic dictionaries from OUP, this feature is known as the 'Oxford Genie'. In the *MED*, it is called the 'QuickFind' feature (see Figure 4.4). Longman calls this feature 'pop-up'. On some dictionaries, the learner can also listen to the word pronounced as the cursor is moved over it. Many learners find this feature invaluable, and it effectively turns a web page into a multimedia experience. This feature also works with email, PowerPoint, Acrobat and Word.

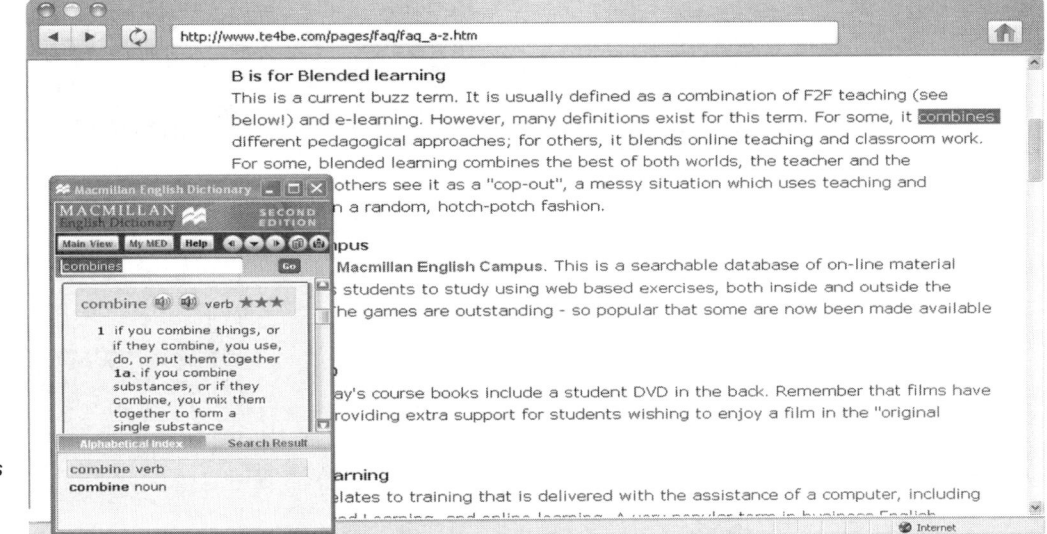

Figure 4.4
The QuickFind feature on the Macmillan English Dictionary.
It recognizes combines *as an inflected form of* combine *and takes the user to the entry for* combine.

Using a CD-ROM dictionary while writing

CD-ROM dictionaries may contain tools which can help learners with their writing. On the *Cambridge Advanced Learner's Dictionary*, one such feature is the SUPERwrite function. It can be opened on-screen while learners compose an essay in their word processor; they can check for meaning and also look for words with related meanings, in order to vary their choice of language (see Figure 4.5).

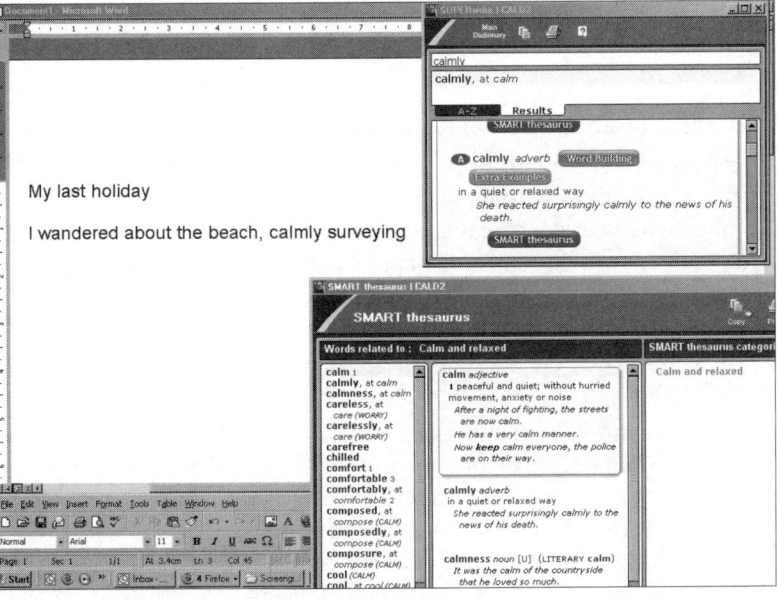

Figure 4.5
The SUPERwrite facility on the Cambridge Advanced Learner's Dictionary. *The learner is checking words related to* calm, *and has clicked on the SMART thesaurus entry.*

On the *Longman Dictionary of Contemporary English* CD-ROM, the Writing Assistant offers help to learners engaged in writing by helping them check that they have chosen the word with the correct meaning, and showing alternatives.

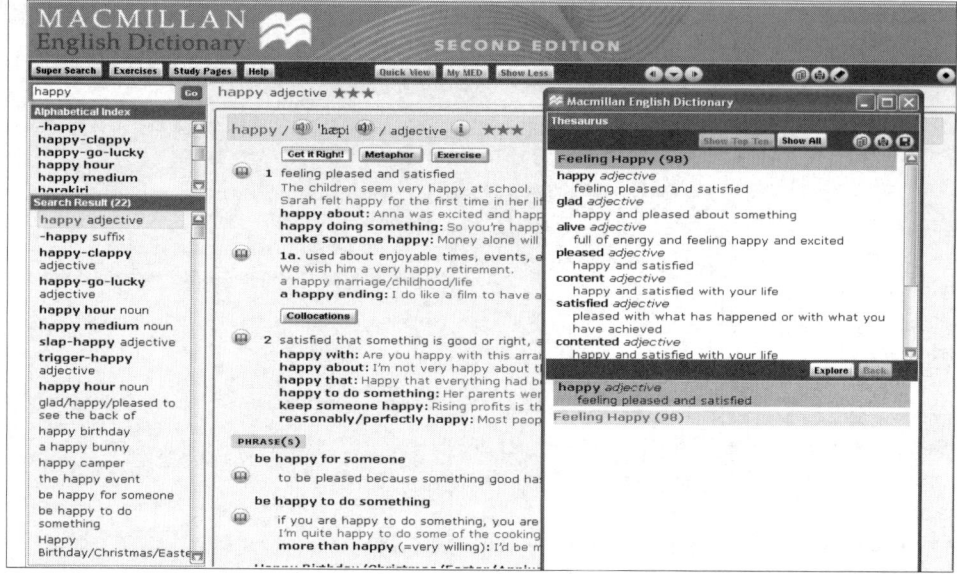

Figure 4.6
The thesaurus
feature of the
Macmillan English
Dictionary *showing*
the Top Ten
synonyms for the
word happy

The thesaurus feature

A useful feature is one whereby the dictionary search facility brings together related words. On the *Cambridge Advanced Learner's Dictionary*, this is called the 'SMART Thesaurus', and helps learners locate synonyms and words related to a particular topic. On the *Macmillan English Dictionary*, users are shown the Top Ten synonyms or related words and, if they wish, they can explore other alternatives and related categories by using the Show All or Explore buttons. All the words within a CD-ROM dictionary are hyperlinked, which means that clicking on a word in the definition takes you to the dictionary entry for that word.

Additional features of CD-ROM dictionaries

Unlike print dictionaries, CD-ROMs are not constrained by space. CD-ROMs as a result often contain extra material the print version does not include. This may include full inflections, additional examples and etymologies. CD-ROMs include photographs, animations, video clips and maps. Illustrations of any type are usually grouped by topic, and typical categories include fruit and vegetables, sports, parts of a car, clothes and so on. The illustrations are usually interactive: when learners move the mouse over the pictures, the name of the word is displayed, and this is linked to its definition in the dictionary.

Some electronic dictionaries allow learners the chance to annotate a word. This means they can add their own, personalized notes to a dictionary entry, which are then backed up onto the user's hard drive and are displayed every time the dictionary is started. On the *MED* CD-ROM, users can copy and paste lists of words into other applications, such as Word, and can create their own glossaries. Most dictionaries also contain exercises. These may be interactive or printable as a pdf.

Online dictionaries

Learner's dictionaries on the Web

Many dictionaries are now available online. Most, but not all, are free to access. These include learner's dictionaries, specialist dictionaries and translating dictionaries. Some of these have been created specifically for the Web, and have no paper-based equivalent. On the other hand, amongst the most popular learners' dictionaries are online versions of those already existing in print. Major ELT publishers usually have an online version of a learner's dictionary on their website, often giving sample features from the CD-ROM version. Online dictionaries are often supported by resources such as downloadable worksheets, interactive games and new words. Some online dictionaries offer the chance to listen to a word. Publishers' online dictionaries include:

- Cambridge Dictionaries online
  http://dictionary.cambridge.org
  This site includes the possibility of searching several dictionaries, such as the *Cambridge Dictionary of Phrasal Verbs* and the *Cambridge Dictionary of Idioms.*

- *Longman Dictionary of Contemporary English* online
  http://www.ldoceonline.com
  This includes the pronunciation of selected examples of words and sentences (see Figure 4.7).

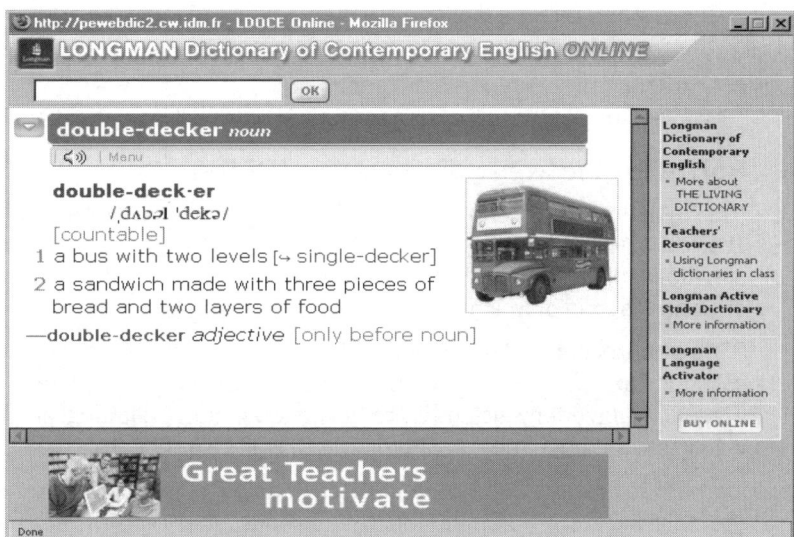

Figure 4.7
Longman
Dictionary of
Contemporary
English *online*

- *Macmillan English Dictionary Online (MEDO)*
  http://www.macmillandictionary.com/online
  You receive a free subscription to the *MEDO*, which includes audio, when you buy a copy of the *Macmillan English Dictionary*. If you mistype a word, you get a page of 'near matches', which may well include the actual word you were looking for.

- *Oxford Advanced Learner's Dictionary* online *(OALD)*
  http://www.oup.com/elt/catalogue/teachersites/oald7/?cc=nl

In the online *OALD*, the search result of many words includes a drop-down menu. This enables users to go directly to a particular idiom or expression. For example, the drop-down menu for the entry *kiss* includes *air kiss, the kiss principle, kiss of life* and so on.

Specialist dictionaries

The many specialist dictionaries on the Web cover areas such as agriculture, arts, business, construction, engineering, finance, IT, law, marketing, medicine, music and science. Specialist dictionaries are mainly aimed at native speakers or advanced-level learners, and will be less concerned with having a limited, easy-to-use defining vocabulary. A further difference in an online specialist dictionary is that the definitions may be hyperlinked.

For a free multilingual dictionary on the Web, see http://en.wiktionary.org/wiki/Main_Page.

Translation dictionaries

There are several types of translation dictionaries on the Web, ranging from simple word lists to more sophisticated dictionaries which allow you to type in text for translation. The latter usually come with a proviso that the translation is not a substitute for a human translator. Translation dictionaries are especially popular with lower-level learners and are especially effective for situations where you need to know the specific word. Some examples of popular translation dictionaries are:

- Leo: http://dict.leo.org
  A popular German–English translation dictionary.

- Word Reference: http://www.wordreference.com
  The Word Reference dictionaries are free online translation dictionaries.
  The Spanish, French and the Italian dictionaries are the most popular.

- LexiCool: http://www.lexicool.com
  A collection of bilingual and multilingual dictionaries on the Web.

Portable electronic dictionaries (PEDs)

A portable electronic dictionary (or PED) is a modern, lightweight and fashionable gadget. There is a range of different types of PED. A typical PED used by learners contains a bi-directional dictionary, eg English–Polish, Polish–English. Many PEDs contain a range of dictionaries, one of which may be a monolingual English learner's dictionary.

PEDs often include extensive vocabularies, grammar references, phrase banks containing colloquial expressions and common phrases, and other information, such as lists of irregular verbs. Many include a pronunciation feature, allowing learners to listen to words in English, although the sound quality may well be inferior to a CD-ROM dictionary.

Many PEDs have additional features, such as offering example sentences in English, the facility to store words, test activities and exam exercises. Games are common, such as hangman and bingo. Some machines allow users to swap memory 'cards', so a completely different dictionary (French–Polish / Polish–French, Business English, etc) can be loaded onto the same device. A pocket translator may contain features such as 'text-to-speech' technologies where learners type in a phrase in order to hear it.

In order to use a PED or translator, the learner simply uses the keyboard to input the word he or she is looking for. The screen then displays the definition or the translation. Some machines have handwriting-recognition software installed.

Concordancers

A concordancer is a tool which can be used to search, access and analyze language from a corpus. A corpus is a collection of written and spoken language stored on a computer, used for language research and writing dictionaries. Today's dictionaries are all based on corpora. Among the many corpora available is the British National Corpus, or BNC. This is a 100-million-word collection which contains samples of written and spoken language.

Concordance software searches a corpus and displays the results of your search: a list of all the occurrences of a certain word in a text or corpus. The word is shown, together with the context in which it appears. This context is usually about seven or eight words to the left and right of the word, which is called the *node* (see Figure 4.8). This common type of display is known as KWIC – key word in context. Originally used in text analysis, it is possible to set the number of words you would like to see displayed on either side of the target item.

1320	taste it is that such	poor	cattle always have in their mouths
948	of sparing the	poor	child the inheritance of any part of
778	small property of my	poor	father, whom I never saw – so long
1870	desolate, while your	poor	heart pined away, weep for it
947	Miss, if the	poor	lady had suffered so intensely
1884	the love of my	poor	mother hid his torture from me
1615	stockings, and all his	poor	tatters of clothes, had, in a long
1577	faded away into a	poor	weak stain. So sunken and
1001	on your way to the	poor	wronged gentleman, and, with a

Figure 4.8
An example of a concordance line for the word poor *occurring in* A Tale of Two Cities *(Charles Dickens)*

There are a number of well-known concordancers:

- WordSmith from OUP: http://www.lexically.net/wordsmith
- MonoConc from the publisher Athelstan: http://athel.com
  Like WordSmith, it is an inexpensive and easy-to-use concordancer designed mainly for teachers and researchers rather than dictionary publishers.
- Sketch Engine: http://www.sketchengine.co.uk
  This is fast and powerful. Unlike MonoConc and WordSmith, there is no software to install, as it runs online. Users need to take out a low-cost subscription for non-commercial individual use. It comes preloaded with the BNC for English and several other corpora in different languages. Using Sketch Engine requires a broadband connection.

There are a number of concordancers available on the Web. These usually have limited functionality, but nevertheless your learners can perform searches and the software produces a sample concordance line. Try:

- http://www.lextutor.ca/concordancers
- http://sara.natcorp.ox.ac.uk/lookup.html
- http://ysomeya.hp.infoseek.co.jp
  This is based on a small corpus, and can be useful for those who need English for business purposes.
- http://132.208.224.131/concordancers/concord_e.html
  This concordancer allows you to choose between several corpora.

There is a lot of information on how to use concordancers at Tim John's website: http://www.eisu.bham.ac.uk/johnstf/timconc.htm.

Opportunities and issues

Using CD-ROM and online dictionaries

Many of the advantages listed below are equally applicable to online and CD-ROM dictionaries, such as the search facilities. By raising awareness of electronic dictionaries in general, you may indirectly be helping your learners become more autonomous. Once learners are aware of the many features of a dictionary, they may feel encouraged to spend time exploring the language further by using the hyperlinks, doing exercises and so on. With a CD-ROM and an online dictionary, you can look up a word more quickly, which may of itself encourage frequent use. Of course, using both these tools assumes the major constraint that users need to have a computer and/or an Internet connection.

One of the main opportunities of CD-ROM dictionaries is in relation to pronunciation. During a class, you can keep a running list of words which learners find difficult to pronounce. You can photocopy and distribute the list, or write it on the board at the end of the lesson. Learners can then listen to the CD-ROM and practise their pronunciation after the lesson. One important issue here is the availability of headphones and microphones for learners. Using a CD-ROM for listening is best done with headphones, and to benefit from the pronunciation-practice feature, computers need to be set up with a microphone. In our experience, these two items are often missing in self-access centres.

Incorporating the pronunciation opportunities of a CD-ROM is a good example of blended learning in action. In the face-to-face part of the lesson, learners discuss the subject of a classroom talk with you. During the preparation and rehearsal stage, they can check the pronunciation of key words on a CD-ROM monolingual English dictionary. This can be done at a computer in the classroom, at a self-access centre or at home. Finally, again in the class, they deliver their presentation to you and the group. Their talk, we would argue, is improved due to work done on the computer.

The feature which allows learners to use a minimized version of the dictionary in conjunction with a web page (eg the 'QuickFind' on the *MED*) offers learners a new tool to help them while reading. It gives them access to meaning on demand without leaving their browser. This feature is popular with Business English learners browsing their company website in English, or EAP learners faced with a complex text on the Web. Using this feature of a dictionary arms learners with a further reading strategy, albeit specific to on-screen reading.

With the 'SUPERwrite' tool, learners can develop a new and useful writing strategy. By accessing synonyms and checking both spelling and meaning while composing in a Word document, they are effectively monitoring their own work, in advance of their own editing later.

The features contained within CD-ROM dictionaries especially can be quite diverse.

- The definitions can be easily copied and pasted into a Word document. This means you can quickly prepare a worksheet containing a mini-glossary, a set of words plus their definitions, which could be used in support of a reading text.
- An online dictionary can be used anywhere the learner has an Internet connection. A key advantage of using an online dictionary, unlike a CD-ROM or print dictionary, is that it can be kept up to date. New words come into the language at a great rate, possibly as many as three to four a day. This makes online dictionaries a perfect companion to a learner's paper-based dictionary or CD-ROM dictionary. An online

version has no restrictions on space, but can continue to grow as new entries are added at any time. The compilers are free to give as many examples of words as they wish.

- Electronic dictionaries can generally also use colour in the text without the cost constraints found in paper dictionaries. Colour can be an effective way of highlighting the differences between groups of words. This can add to the appeal of both CD-ROM and online dictionaries, particularly for visual learners.

One way of familiarizing learners with online dictionaries is to exploit the 'Word of the day' or 'Word of the week' feature. This is an email service which the learners can subscribe to, just like an email newsletter. A word and its definition are emailed to the learners daily or weekly. Learners can then report back to the class on the words they have received.

An important consideration is that an online dictionary must be appropriate to the needs and level of your learners. In this respect, translation dictionaries may be especially useful for beginners and elementary learners and those needing a one-to-one equivalent of a specialist term, such as a Business English or ESP learner.

See *Practical activities* (page 63) for an activity which explores these ideas and can be used as the basis of a learner training session.

Using portable electronic dictionaries

Some advantages of using electronic dictionaries include the fact they are portable, and can be taken on trips, used in lectures and so on. This allows for 'just-in-time' access and means learners can use them to access meaning on the move – in museums, while shopping; the possibilities are endless.

Speed is often cited by learners as a major reason why they use their PED – they can locate the words faster than looking in a bilingual paperback dictionary. They are also popular with many learners due to their ease of use and their perceived low cost. The features such as storing of words, self-testing and playing games are all mentioned by teachers who frequently encourage learners to review and recycle new vocabulary. Another reason learners like PEDs is because they can contain more than one dictionary – a bilingual and a monolingual dictionary, for instance. This allows users to jump from one dictionary to another. For example, they can look up a difficult word in a definition provided by a monolingual dictionary in a bilingual dictionary.

There are some caveats. Learners may become over-reliant on the translation aspect, and ignore the learning strategy of guessing meaning from context. When writing, they may produce inappropriate language. These disadvantages are similar to the overuse of bilingual dictionaries. Encouraging a second check in a monolingual dictionary is to be recommended, especially when learners are producing essays.

Many teachers complain that their learners ignore the advice given in a learner training session on good reading strategies, and simply turn to their translators. Sometimes, a classroom is punctuated by the sound of bleeping noises or digital voices pronouncing a word. Are learners being rude? Should they be allowed to use their PEDs in class? Rather than allowing indiscriminate use of such dictionaries, it is arguably better to negotiate with learners a way of limiting their use. Agree to have some lessons when they do not have access to these, such as a fluency lesson. Remind them that they need to consider that over-reliance on translators may not be helpful, as such tools may not be allowed in an examination.

Using concordancers

One opportunity afforded by concordancers is that they allow learners to meet words in a range of different and authentic contexts. Concordancers have been useful for ELT materials writers, enabling them to study the way language works and to include more authentic examples in coursebooks.

You can encourage learners to research the language through consulting a concordancer in what has been called DDL, or data-driven learning. In one online concordancer, learners can write or paste their own text into a window, select a concordancer from a drop-down menu, and then check their use of unfamiliar words or structures. If you want to teach learners how to use concordancers to edit their written work, you can use: http://www.lextutor.ca/grammar_tester. If you go to the homepage of the same website, you can find several useful authoring tools. One such tool allows learners to click on any word in a text and study it through a concordancer and an online dictionary. Learners can even insert their own texts and edit them.

 The use of a concordancer can help learners gain insights into particular aspects of vocabulary, such as collocation or word frequency. Rather than simply giving learners an answer, the learner can be engaged in working out rules from the results of concordance lines. This possibility has been described by Jane Willis, who explores the use of consciousness-raising activities based on concordance lines in *A Framework for Task-based Learning* (Longman, 1996). Learners can look up common mistakes and areas of difficulty, such as the use of articles (*customers* vs *the customer*). Taking the example of collocation, you can prepare a worksheet using a concordance line for a key word. You delete the key word and challenge the learners to work together to guess the original word. As a follow-up, learners can themselves visit an online concordancer and create a similar exercise for their classmates.

One key issue is whether the centre you work in has access to a concordancer or not. In our experience, these are not very common in schools. It is still viable to give learners a flavour of what is involved in using such a tool by using a concordancer on the Internet, and the practical idea in the final section of this chapter can be used with an online concordancer.

One problem with concordancers is that some learners such as lower intermediate learners may find it daunting to look at a page full of data which may also contain a lot of new words. Some may have never analyzed language before. A possible solution is to start by giving learners an edited version of the concordance lines in which difficult words and complex sentences have been removed. This will introduce them to the use of concordancers gradually.

Practical activities

CD-ROM dictionary demonstration

Aim: to demonstrate the features of CD-ROM dictionaries

Level: intermediate and higher

Interaction: Step 2 is a teacher presentation, using an electronic projector; Step 3 involves learners working at workstations or in pairs

Technology: CD-ROM dictionaries; a similar lesson can be run using online dictionaries if the classroom has an Internet connection

Rationale: Learners often use a bilingual dictionary due to unfamiliarity with other options. Knowledge of a CD-ROM dictionary can encourage learners to explore features of the CD and build up their confidence in using them. Learners cannot realistically look at all the features of all dictionaries, so a teacher demo can point them towards the most useful features for their needs.

Before class: You should familiarize yourself with the features you wish to demonstrate. The electronic projector needs to be set up. If learners are going to use the disks, the CD-ROM dictionaries need to be pre-loaded. If using online dictionaries, you need the relevant URLs, which can be bookmarked in advance.

Procedure:

1 Ask learners to share their experiences of using a CD-ROM dictionary.

2 Demonstrate some key features of a specific disk or disks, such as searching for a word. Point out that searching on a CD-ROM dictionary is faster than using a hard-copy dictionary. Demonstrate the pronunciation feature. Choose a word such as *banana* or *advertisement* to demonstrate the US/UK difference. Show learners how to record themselves. Show any other useful features, such as the QuickFind, etc.

3 At this point, learners should get hands-on experience of using the CD-ROMs. They can browse the dictionary freely, or do a more controlled task, such as taking the CD-ROM guided tour. Alternatively, set one of the three task variations below.

Variations:

1 Give each learner a difficult, relevant text. They summarize the text in 200 words. In order to prepare the summary, learners use a CD-ROM dictionary to look up the unknown words. When they have finished, debrief the task: did they find the electronic dictionary useful? Which features of the CD-ROM were useful?

2 Divide the class into small groups. Assign each group to a different CD-ROM dictionary. They meet in groups to discuss what they liked about the disks.

3 Devise a CD-ROM treasure hunt. This is a quiz designed to encourage learners to look at different features of the disk, such as the maps, the visuals, the advanced search features, etc.

Exploring word frequency

Aim: to raise awareness of word frequency

Level: intermediate and higher

Interaction: individuals/pairs

Technology: CD-ROM dictionaries

Rationale: Learners are often unaware of the importance of knowing about word frequency. They will therefore be unable to sort new lexis into useful categories, such as words for productive and receptive purposes. They may not know about the relative frequency of similar words, such as *let* and *permit*, which is important for writing.

Before class: Photocopy the worksheet (see page 142). Take in hard copies of the *MED* to class. Alternatively, learners can go to the CD-ROM or *MED* online, if available. The CD-ROM allows you to search for words by frequency

Procedure:

1 Explain the star-rating system used in *MED* (see the worksheet).

2 Issue the worksheet and get learners to guess the answers. Tell learners that the list of five words contains at least one word from each of the four frequency bands.

3 Learners compare their answers with a partner.

4 Pairs report back on any differences.

5 Refer learners to the *Macmillan English Dictionary* in a range of formats in order to check and compare their answers.

6 As a class, deal with feedback on the task. (See below for answers.) Ask learners whether they were correct or not. Also ask about the implications of the task. For example, if they do not know a high-frequency word, they need to study it and add it into their lexical notebooks. The star system helps learners to decide if the word should be part of their productive or receptive vocabulary. Also mention the need to mark words with N (noun), V (verb), etc when they record them in their notebooks.

Answers: cast * / cancer *** / exposure ** / hassle * / mint (no star)

Variations: Adapt the worksheet for use with other monolingual English dictionaries used in your school. Point out that different learner's dictionaries deal with frequency in different ways, eg Longman dictionaries differentiate frequency of written and spoken English; OUP provide a list of frequent words, the Oxford 3000™.

Dictionary comparison

Aim: to raise awareness of the range of dictionaries available on CD-ROM

Level: intermediate and higher

Interaction: groupwork and feedback

Rationale: Learners are often unaware of the features and benefits of using a monolingual English dictionary and the types of media (CD-ROM, Internet) available.

Technology: CD-ROM dictionaries

Before class: Ensure that you have the relevant dictionary sets on hand, plus computers with access to the Web and the CD-ROM dictionaries loaded. Photocopy the worksheet (see page 143).

Procedure:

1 Write up some words on the board. These could be new words you wish to pre-teach, or words from a recent class which you have chosen to recycle. Divide the class into four sub-groups and ask each group to find out the meaning of the words.
Group 1 uses an electronic translator or bilingual dictionary.
Group 2 uses a print monolingual English learner's dictionary.
Group 3 uses a CD-ROM dictionary.
Group 4 uses a web-based dictionary.

2 Issue the worksheet 'Using dictionaries' (see page 143). Each group completes the relevant section.

3 The class meets as a whole. Each group reports back on their sections, covering the pros and cons. Others can complete their worksheets by taking notes on the back of each report.

4 Ask learners what they have learned in this class. Open up a discussion about the various media used: do learners have any preferences? Will they take any action, such as visiting an online dictionary or buying an English–English learner's dictionary?

Using web dictionaries to explore neologisms

Aim: to raise awareness of one of the features of online learner's dictionaries, namely the inclusion of new words

Level: intermediate and higher

Interaction: individual or pairs; feedback to the group

Technology: online dictionaries

Rationale: Many learners own dictionaries which are quite old. It is useful for them to know that they can supplement their dictionary with a web-based dictionary which is more likely to contain new words (neologisms).

Before class: Check the Internet connection; bookmark the URLs.

Procedure:

1 Ask learners to guess how many new words enter the language every day. Linguists have calculated that on average the figure may be as high as three or four.

2 Issue a number of words on cards (see below for examples) and ask learners to check if they are in their own print dictionary or not. Include your own cards which show words which have come up in your lesson, such as jargon or new words.

3 Learners go the Internet and check which words are in an online dictionary.

4 Learners report back on which words they found.

5 Discuss what the implications of this task are. For example, they may decide to add the web addresses of one or more online dictionary to their favourites list.

bling	weapons of mass destruction	copyleft	wifi
phishing	to google	metrosexual	blog

Mapping words

Aim: to raise awareness of what is involved in 'knowing' a word

Level: intermediate and higher

Interaction: pairs

Technology: CD-ROM dictionary

Rationale: Learners often write a one-to-one translation of a word. They are often unaware of just how much is involved in knowing a word. This could be a good opportunity to introduce learners to the concept of collocation and connotation.

Before class: Decide which disks you wish to use, and ensure they are loaded on the computers available. Photocopy the worksheet (see page 144) onto OHTs if learners can use an OHP in Step 3.

Procedure:

1 Remind learners what is involved in 'knowing' a word. This could include meaning, how to use it, forming derivatives (noun/adjective/adverb, etc), understanding connotation, using collocation, and pronunciation. Demonstrate how to build up a 'word map', eg a word map for *economy* should include *economic, economical, economist* and any useful collocations such as *economically sound, economically viable,* etc.

2 Issue the worksheet (see page 144). Learners in pairs choose a word to explore. Learners research their word using the CD-ROM. They draw a 'word map' of their word, eg in EAP and Business English, a key word from their subject area or field. This can be done on OHT transparency.

3 Learners present their 'word map' to the group. If possible, take photocopies of their map for distribution to the other learners.

Follow up: This activity could lead into more learner training on how to store words in their vocabulary notebooks, eg by concept. Learners can create word maps for other key words; they can create their own meaningful sentences with some of the new expressions or collocations presented by others in the class; they can explore synonyms of their chosen word using the Visual Thesaurus website at http://www.visualthesaurus.com.

Classroom-based research

Acknowledgement for this idea: Hilary Nesi

Aim: to get learners to consider the advantages and the disadvantages of using PEDs

Level: intermediate and higher

Interaction: pairs or small groups

Rationale: to promote discussion and raise awareness of appropriate and inappropriate uses of PEDs

Technology: personal electronic dictionaries

Before class: This lesson is designed to work with groups where learners bring their own PEDs to class. Photocopy one worksheet (see page 145) for each pair or small group. Check you have a note of some of the benefits and drawbacks (see checklist below).

Procedure:

1 Issue the worksheet (see page 145). Learners work in pairs or small groups to compare the features of their PEDs. Learners in multilingual classes should work in groups with learners from different countries.

2 Groups present their findings to the whole class. Be ready to provide any important points that your learners have not considered (see below).

PEDs	
Features	Translation from English to another language
	English–English dictionary
	Examples of use
	Example phrases
	Idioms
	Synonyms
	UK and US pronunciation
	A review system; facility to create wordlists
	Wordlists for exams
	Other features
Benefits	Cost
	Speed
	Portability
Drawbacks	They encourage the idea of a one-to-one meaning relationship between different languages.
	They are not always good for productive purposes.
	They may create dependence.
	Screen display size may be small, so you cannot see a complete entry all at once.

Using a concordancer for language research

Acknowledgement for this idea: Anna Calvi

Aim: to show how a concordancer can be used for language research

Level: intermediate and higher

Interaction: pairs

Rationale: Learners are likely to remember a rule if they are involved in the process of working it out. This activity is good for raising awareness of recurring errors, such as the use of articles and confusion over countable vs uncountable nouns. Learners may well be largely unaware of concordancers, and may be inspired to use them later as part of their continued language study.

Technology: online concordancers

Before class: Print out the concordance lines for the language point to be studied; in this example, one concordance line for *customers* and one for *the customers*. The concordance lines may need slightly simplifying, which can be done in a word processor. Make a list of problematic language areas which you would like the learners to research later in the lesson. Make a note of the URL of the online concordancer you wish learners to use.

Procedure:

1 Pose the problem: 'When do we use *customers* and when do we use *the customers*?' Issue the two concordance lines you have printed out and ask learners to study the examples.

2 Invite one pair of learners to explain the difference. Typical answers will distinguish between general uses and specific uses of the term.

3 Learners in pairs visit an online concordancer and type in another word or phrase. These could be areas which you feel learners would benefit from such as: *few* vs *a few* / *little* vs *a little* / *data* vs *datas* / *persons* vs *people*.

4 Learners report back, explaining what they think is the difference between the forms being contrasted

Follow up: Suggest to learners that they add a concordance URL to their favourites.

Variations: This activity is very useful for helping learners distinguish between easily confused tenses, such as the present simple vs the present continuous.

Case study

Case study:
Equipping a self-access centre with CD-ROM dictionaries

John works as a director of studies in a language school in Oxford, UK. The centre decided to invest in a small self-access centre by buying twelve computers. John was asked to buy in CD-ROM dictionaries and load them onto the computers. He was not sure whether to choose one dictionary and load it onto all the computers. The advantage here was perhaps simplifying things for the teachers and learners, as they could access the same disk on all the machines. He investigated the possibility of using a network version. He finally decided that he would buy three copies each of the English–English dictionaries from the main UK publishers: *Cambridge Advanced Learner's Dictionary, Longman Dictionary of Contemporary English, Macmillan English Dictionary for Advanced Learners* and *Oxford Advanced Learner's Dictionary* on CD-ROM. He felt that there were benefits in taking each class into the centre and doing a task to compare the features of these four CD-ROMs. He was happy that all the computers were linked to a central printer. He made a note to remind the school manager that they needed to buy headphones and external microphones for the computers.

After six months, John asked the learners in the school to give feedback on the dictionaries available in the self-access centre. The learners liked the fact that they could choose to use a CD-ROM dictionary which complemented their own print dictionary. However, the lower-level class had not used the CD-ROMs because they thought the dictionaries in the self-access centre were too difficult. John decided he needed to buy and install an elementary level dictionary, and ordered the *Oxford Essential Dictionary* (OUP) from his regular supplier.

Office software includes email clients, word processors, databases, spreadsheets and presentation programs. A combination of these programs will be installed on most computers in workplaces and other institutions. Because of their ubiquity, they are sometimes overlooked as teaching and learning tools. This chapter looks at how two of these programs, word-processing and presentation software, can be integrated into a language course. This integration can be seamless, and the use of such programs can enable teachers to deliver blended-learning courses, with learners and teachers using these programs inside and outside the classroom.

Using word-processing software

A word processor is the piece of software that the majority of computer users are familiar with. It is present in some form on most computers around the world. It allows users to enter and format text, which can then be printed onto paper, and is used in offices to write letters and reports, in schools and universities to write essays and academic papers, and in homes to produce many text-based documents.

The most common word-processor program is Microsoft Word, which comes as a stand-alone program or as part of the Microsoft Office suite of programs. A specially priced version of this package is available for teachers working in the state sector. Another popular program is WordPerfect, which comes as part of the WordPerfect Office suite. Both of these are available for Windows and Macintosh computers. Microsoft Works, which is often pre-installed on new Windows computers, also includes a cut-down version of Microsoft Word. Apple's own word-processor programs are available as part of the iWork and AppleWorks packages. Free office software is available from OpenOffice.org, which includes a word-processing program called Write. This comes in Windows and Macintosh versions and is compatible with Microsoft file formats.

Text typed into a word-processor program can be edited and formatted using a number of simple tools. Text can be copied or cut from one location within a document and pasted into another part of the document or into a separate document. This is done using commands under the Edit menu or by using buttons on the toolbar. You can also use the keyboard: press the *Ctrl* key (⌘ for Macs) at the same time as the *X, C* and *V* keys for 'cut', 'copy' and 'paste' respectively. You can also use different fonts and modify the size of the text to differentiate between headings and main text, or if you are designing something such as a poster.

The files produced by word-processing programs can easily be transferred from computer to computer via networks, email or other portable storage media. Hard copies can quickly be produced using a printer. Errors can be corrected, and amendments can be made quickly and easily. You should save documents for future use or reference. In some institutions, computers are connected via a network, and learners can create a folder on a central server and store documents there. The alternative for learners using a communal computer is to save documents to a portable memory storage such as a writable CD-ROM or a USB flash drive.

Although most word-processor files are compatible with each other, older programs are often unable to open files created in newer versions. If you do not know the version of the program you are using, check by clicking on the Help menu (the Apple or program menu for

Macs) then selecting *About*. This will display the version number and the date the program was launched. If you and your learners are using different versions of a program, save all documents in a format that will be recognised by the oldest version.

Using presentation software

These programs allow you to prepare a presentation made up of electronic slides, which can contain text, pictures and diagrams, hyperlinks to documents, web pages and multimedia elements such as audio clips. Once the presentation has been prepared, the program is switched to View mode, and the presenter can advance through the presentation by clicking a mouse button or pressing a computer key.

The most popular program is PowerPoint from Microsoft; it is part of the Microsoft Office suite of programs or it can be purchased separately. Alternatives are Presentations in the WordPerfect Office suite; Keynote for Macintosh computers, which is included in iWork; and the OpenOffice program Impress.

In situations where the presenter and audience are together in the same room, the image from the computer screen is projected onto a display screen using a data projector. With smaller audiences, the projector can be dispensed with and the slides displayed on the screen of a laptop computer. Another mode of use is a guided presentation in which there is no presenter, but the audience of one clicks through the presentation by following prompts on the screen. This type of presentation can be accessed from a website or intranet. In this context, options and choices can be offered to make the presentation less linear. Some presentation programs allow a voiceover to be recorded and the presentation programmed to run by itself.

Microsoft provide a free program that allows you to view a presentation created in PowerPoint even if you do not have the complete PowerPoint program installed on your computer. This can be downloaded from Microsoft's website (http://www.microsoft.com/downloads).

Like word-processing software, knowing how to use presentation programs is fast becoming a standard skill. Most competent computer users can learn the basics in a very short time.

The instructions below give a very brief step-by-step guide to making a simple presentation with Microsoft PowerPoint. The other programs mentioned in this section are very similar in their operation.

1 Open the program.

2 Select Blank presentation and click on OK.

3 In the New Slide box, select the Title Slide and click on OK.

4 Click on the slide on the right of the screen and type in your title. In this example, the presentation is called 'Working in England'. The sub-title is 'The results of our research'. (See Figure 5.1.)

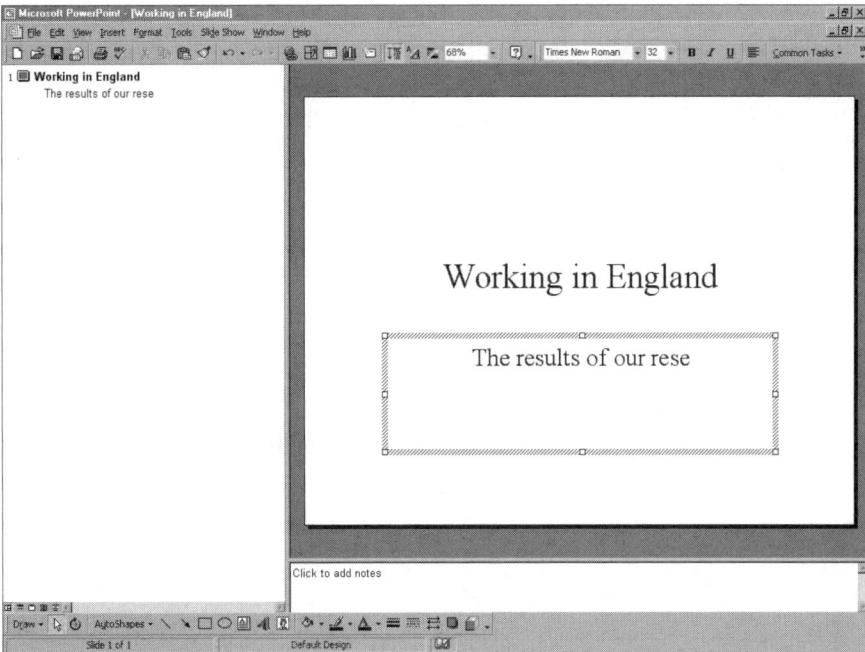

Figure 5.1
Insert a title.

5 When you are ready, click the Insert menu and select New Slide …

6 In the New Slide box, select the Bulleted List and click on OK.

7 Type in a title for your new slide, then click next to the first bullet and type in the main sections of your presentation. Press Enter on the keyboard to start a new bullet point. (See Figure 5.2.)

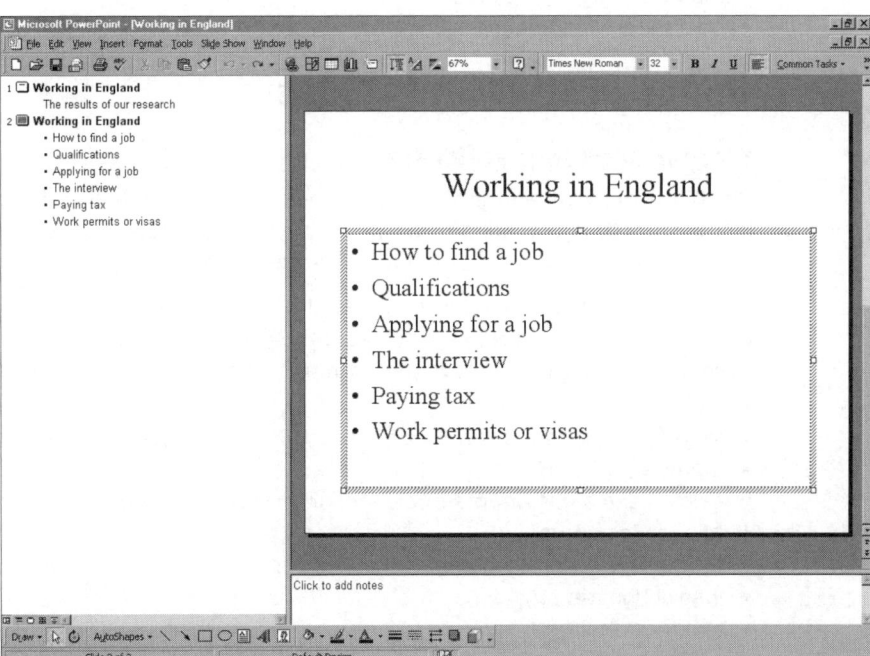

Figure 5.2
Insert bullet
points.

8   Continue to add slides until you have completed your presentation.

9   To run your presentation, click the Slide Show menu and select View Show or press the F5 key. The first slide will fill the computer screen. (See Figure 5.3.)

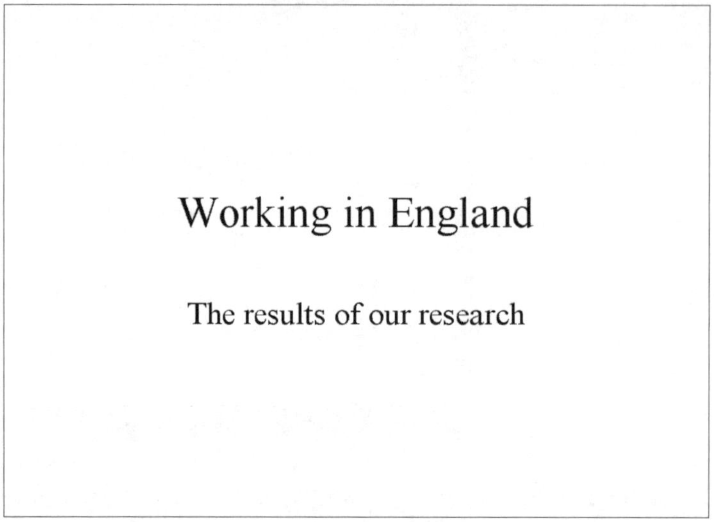

Figure 5.3
The first slide
as displayed in
presentation
mode.

Working in England

The results of our research

10   To progress through the slides, you can press the PgUp or right cursor key on the keyboard, or click the mouse. If you want to go backwards to an earlier slide, press PgDn or the left cursor key.

The basic rules for designing PowerPoint slides are the same as those for old-fashioned OHTs:

• keep text to a minimum
• make text big enough to read
• be careful with colours, eg do not put red text on an orange background.

Opportunities and issues

Word-processing software

One of the main advantages of word-processing software is that computer-literate learners are bound to be familiar with this type of program, so they will be able to focus on the language without any significant software learning curve to slow them down.

The ease with which texts can be created, edited, copied, distributed, shared and finally printed makes word-processor software the ideal tool for a wide range of activities. Learners who need to improve their writing skills can use word processors for:

• letters
• reports (business, scientific or the results of other forms of research)
• memos
• essays and assignments for school or university courses
• academic papers
• articles for school or company newsletters
• instruction manuals
• text for websites
• creative writing.

Other activities which are more language focused but can have a written outcome include:

- vocabulary storage
- class newsletters
- diaries
- stories
- poetry and song lyrics
- scripts for radio or TV programmes
- preparing postings for a blog (see Chapter 9)
- creating exercises for peers.

Writing is often an individual activity. This means that you can set writing tasks to be undertaken by your learners outside the classroom. The completed tasks can be emailed to you or stored in a location on an institution's computer network which is accessible to both you and your learners. Feedback on such a task can be also done electronically.

However, learners using word processors can sometimes be seduced by the speed at which they can enter text. You should encourage them to reread for errors of all types. Extensive cutting and pasting while editing a document can also result in loose odds and ends of words or sentences that can only be picked out by thorough proofreading. Keyboard layout varies from country to country, and touch typists will need to be reminded to take care when using an unfamiliar layout.

Word processors also contain language tools which learners can use for editing. For example, the spell-checker feature can be set to check for British or American spellings, depending on the target type of English. Encourage your learners to make use of this feature, although you should warn them that it is no substitute for a thorough proofread, as, for example, it will not pick up errors with homophones (eg *it's/its, their/there*). Grammar checkers should also be approached with caution. In fact, it is often better to disable this feature of the program. Many CD-ROM dictionaries have a quickfinder feature which allows the dictionary to be integrated with some word-processing programs. If this is available on the computers being used by learners, you need make sure that they know how to use it and insist on the benefits of doing so (see Chapter 4 for more information on CD-ROM dictionaries).

Once work has been completed, checked and submitted, you can make corrections and add comments to your learners' written work by using different coloured fonts, eg the traditional red for highlighting and correcting language mistakes, and another colour for more general comments or suggestions for improving the text. Most word-processor software has special features for dealing with giving feedback. For example, in Word, you can select *Track Changes* from the Tools menu. This allows you to make amendments to the text, with the corrections automatically appearing in a different colour. You can also add comments to the text – for example to explain your corrections or highlight recurring errors – by choosing *Comment* from the Insert menu. It is well worth making yourself familiar with these features.

Different versions of a document can be saved under different names. This allows you to retain the learners' original versions of the documents, as well as the versions with your annotations and any versions rewritten by the learners.

If you want to give feedback in the classroom, the writing tasks can be printed and distributed to all members of the class. If your classroom has a computer linked to a data projector, the word-processor screen can be projected and each writing task edited live with the input of the whole class.

Often the writing activity is not an end in itself. The word processor is simply being used in order to produce a clear printed text which will be used elsewhere. This is the case for class newsletters to be distributed to parents or peers, and for radio or TV scripts which will be used for recording or videoing on another occasion. Groups of learners can use word processors to modify existing texts. This can be done to create exercises for other members of the class (see Chapter 2 for an example activity (*Authentic text gap-fill*)).

Other uses of word-processor programs, such as diaries and vocabulary lists, take advantage of the ease with which text can be cut and pasted, the fact that different colours and fonts can be used for different types of text, the ability of word processors to sort lists alphabetically, and that pictures can be added from clip-art libraries or from websites.

Presentation software

The principle use for presentation software is making presentations. You can use it as a classroom tool to support input lessons for areas such as grammar or functional language. Diagrams, examples or lists of exponents that you would usually draw or write on the board can be replaced by electronic slides. This makes it possible to move backwards and forwards through your slides or introduce elements to an individual slide one at a time. This might be useful, for example, when adding sentences to a time-line. Using the presentation software does not prevent you from also using a traditional board at the same time. If you are projecting your electronic slides onto a white board, you can press the *W* key on the keyboard and the projected screen will become white allowing you to write on the board without interrupting the flow of the prepared presentation or switching off the data projector. (Pressing the *W* key again will return you to the presentation.)

As well as using the software to create presentations for your own purposes, your learners can also use the software to create their own presentations. For some learners, such as those from or about to enter the business world, this is a real-world task. For others, presentations are the culmination of a longer research task or creative task using the language.

If you are unfamiliar with presentation software, there are one or two things to be aware of. New users can get very carried away with all the many options that a program offers them: sound effects, slide transition effects, patterned backgrounds and so on. These not only result in noisy, multi-coloured presentations, but, for language learners, they can absorb vital preparation time which should have been spent focusing on the language to be used.

Presentation software has also become the unwitting parent of many a lazy presentation. The temptation on the part of you and your learners to fill presentation slides with vast tracts of texts which are then read to yawning audiences should be resisted.

As well as the creation and giving of presentations to live audiences, the software can be used to create presentations that run automatically when the file is opened. These can be distributed on CD-ROMs or placed on websites to be viewed online or downloaded and viewed.

An extension of this is to incorporate links into the slides. You can create links to other slides within the presentation or to slides on another presentation stored in a particular place on a computer, a network or a CD-ROM. The result is the presentation can be navigated in a controlled but non-linear manner. This allows you to create a learning maze through which learners can progress on the basis of decisions they are asked to make or questions they have to answer.

Learner mazes can be used for a wide range of subjects, for example, to raise awareness about grammar topics, introduce functional language, help learners to assess their own knowledge about topics such as self-study techniques, and explore a topic such as the customs and traditions of the country where they are staying during their studies. See the case studies below for an example of a maze created using PowerPoint.

Practical activities

Word-processing software

Group writing

Aim: to write a letter or written announcement

Level: intermediate

Interaction: whole class

Technology: word-processor program and data projector

Rationale: Linking a data projector to a computer with word-processor software allows an entire group of learners to work together on a single piece of writing. This can be used as part of a writing skills lesson or course or as a communicative activity. It works best with smaller classes (six to twelve learners).

Before class: This activity focuses on the production of a piece of writing. It therefore works best if your learners have already had experience of writing. You should prepare a writing task with clear objectives and some way of measuring the success of the outcome.

Procedure:

1 Explain that the whole class is going to work together to write a letter (or whatever writing task you have prepared).

2 Brainstorm questions such as who the readers will be, the structure and contents of the text, the most appropriate style and any important vocabulary needed.

3 Ask the class to appoint a scribe, who will sit at the computer and do the typing, and a chairperson, who will moderate the discussion about what to type. If this is a guided activity, you should occupy the position of chairperson.

4 The piece of writing is discussed a sentence at a time. The scribe enters the text using the computer keyboard under instruction from the chairperson. If there is any disagreement about the result, the chairperson allows discussion and the agreed changes are made. Once agreement is reached, the next sentence is discussed.

5 Once the text is complete, it can be printed and distributed to members of the class.

Follow on: This activity can be used as a follow-on to fluency exercises. One example is in Business English, where the class can write up the minutes of a meeting role-play or prepare a public announcement based on the results of a simulated meeting or negotiation.

Class newspaper

Aim: to create a class newspaper

Level: elementary to advanced

Interaction: whole class

Technology: word-processor program and printer

Rationale: This activity is something that can be done with an entire class of young or teenage learners. It can be used as an on-going or end-of-course project. Every member of the class contributes something, and the final product is printed and distributed to family and friends.

Before class: For the activity to work effectively, it is important to assign roles. You can have a class election for these positions or use your judgement and experience of the learners to select class members in advance.

Procedure:

1 Explain that the objective of the project is to produce a class newspaper which can be given to friends and family. Brainstorm the types of things that could appear in such a newspaper, for example:
   - reports on class activities, such as outings or trips
   - reports about what they have learned from or about each other (this is good for a multinational class)
   - stories
   - articles about personal interests or hobbies
   - poems
   - word games
   - pictures and photographs.

2 Appoint an editor or editorial team. Allocate responsibility for creating the content to other members of the class. Make sure everyone has something. This process can be led by you or done as a fluency activity, with the editorial team leading the process.

3 Set a deadline and establish a timetable for creating the content. Allow time for language support and rewrites if necessary. Content can be created as homework, or you can set aside time in each lesson to work on it. At this point, create a project plan with names, responsibilities and deadlines and distribute it to everyone.

4 As the content is created and corrected, the editorial team decide the design and layout of the newspaper. All the elements are collected together, typed up, if necessary, then assembled on a word processor.

5 A first draft is printed and examined by the whole class to find any language mistakes and to discuss whether the layout is clear. They agree on the order in which the content has been placed by the editorial team.

6 Once any changes have been implemented, the final version is printed and each member of the class is provided with copies to give their family and friends.

Follow on: If the learners are together for a long period of time and the first newspaper is judged a success, the project can be repeated with a new editorial team and different people producing different parts of the newspaper each time.

Presentation software

Business presentation

Aim: to give a business presentation

Level: elementary to advanced

Interaction: individual and whole class

Technology: presentation software and data projector

Rationale: For business people, giving presentations is a real-world task. Using a program such as PowerPoint and a data projector, this can be simulated quite closely, especially in front of an audience of their colleagues or peers.

Before class: This activity relies on the learners having experience of using presentation software. If you have a mix of experienced and inexperienced users, pair people up and provide time for peer training. This exercise focuses on the preparation and giving of a presentation. It should be preceded by a lesson focusing on the functional exponents commonly used to structure a business presentation and to handle questions.

Procedure:

1 Explain to the learners that they are going to prepare and give a business presentation. Establish how long each presentation should be (between fifteen and twenty minutes) and emphasize that it should make use of the presentation phrases the class has covered and that they should be ready to field questions at the end. The choice of the topic is up to them, although it should be something they would expect to present as part of their job or be related to their work in some way.

2 Tell your learners that they are going to use PowerPoint (or some similar presentation program) to create the slides for their presentation. Stress that, ultimately, you will be assessing them on the basis of the accuracy and appropriacy of the language they use, so they should spend the majority of their preparation time thinking about what they are going to say and keep the presentation slides minimal. If any learners have company laptops, loaded with an existing company presentation, they can use or adapt that.

3 Give the learners time to prepare. This preparation could be homework or done within a self-study period in the day.

4 Each learner gives their presentation using a computer and data projector to provide the visual support. The presentation can be recorded or videoed to create a permanent record (see Chapter 7). Other members of the class should be encouraged to ask questions.

5 Provide written feedback on the language used by each presenter. You can also provide feedback on the language used on the presentation slides.

Follow on: If you have recorded or videoed the presentations, these recordings can be used for comparison with any subsequent presentations done during the course.

Case studies

Case study 1:
Using word-processing software for vocabulary storage

Chuck teaches classes of adults who take lessons on a weekly basis. An important issue for his learners is storing the vocabulary they have collected and wished to learn. Some of his learners are well organised, while others have no system.

Most of his learners have access to computers at home or at work, as well as portable devices such as palmtop computers. Chuck decided to demonstrate the use of a word-processor program as a possible method for storing vocabulary. He explained to his learners that he was proposing this as one option among others. He emphasised that, if learners were already happy with the way they stored vocabulary, he was not pressurising them to change unnecessarily.

Chuck's demonstration suggested a number of ideas:

- Vocabulary can be organised by topic, with a different page or document for each topic.
- Different colour text or highlighting can be used to classify vocabulary. This can be by parts of speech or how important the word or phrase is for the learner; for example, words and phrases in red need to be learned first. Highlighting can be used to pick out words and phrases in sentences or short pieces of text, for example, to identify phrasal verbs within a context.
- Example sentences, short pieces of text and definitions can be copied and pasted from websites, from other learners' vocabulary lists, from word-processor documents and emails, and from CD-ROM dictionaries.
- Pictures pasted from websites or taken with a digital camera can be used to illustrate vocabulary.
- Hyperlinks can be included in the text to link to definitions from online dictionaries, glossaries on websites or some other online resource that will help to illustrate the vocabulary item's meaning and use.

Figure 5.4 shows part of the example that Chuck used. He explained that this was not a finished page. For example, extra words can be added to the table at any time.

The learners agreed to use the system for a trial period. They found that the advantages were the ability to add and change text quickly and easily. The main disadvantage was that the list could only be consulted using a computer. One learner explained that as his list got bigger, he started to use the word-processor program's Find function to locate words within it. Another regularly used hyperlinks to an online dictionary so he could test himself on the definition of a word before clicking on the link to check his answer.

Market trends

trend (noun) (three stars in MED) – a change or development that occurs over time

Words that often go with *trend*:

current

general

long-term

recent

underlying

Words for describing trends

After a period of stagnation in the euro area the volume of retail trade picked up and grew by 1.6% in the year to April. But surveys of purchasing managers revealed a decline in both services and manufacturing. The index for services rose to 62.1 in August from 60.9 in July. At the same time, the index for manufacturing fell to 54.5 from 56.4.

Verb	Past simple	Past participle	Noun
grow	grew	grown	growth
pick up	picked up	picked up	–
decline	declined	declined	decline
drop	dropped	dropped	drop
fall	fell	fallen	fall

A good place to find trends language:

http://www.economist.com/markets/indicators

Figure 5.4
Example of part
of a vocabulary
list created on
a word processor

Case study 2:
Using presentation software for making interactive mazes

Ellen works in a school with a well-equipped self-access centre. Many of her learners enjoy using computer software to test and expand their knowledge of grammar. Some of them asked Ellen if there was anything they could use on their computers at home. She decided to use Microsoft PowerPoint to create mazes, because PowerPoint presentations are quick and easy to create; they can be burned onto CD-ROMs or emailed to learners; and the person viewing them does not need to have PowerPoint installed on their computer: they can download the viewer (see page 70).

Ellen started with a simple maze which tested her learners' understanding of the use of the present perfect. She chose this because it would not be too complicated to write, create and use. She approached it as a test of her own abilities and whether the result would be something her learners found useful.

First of all, she created the maze on paper, carefully drawing the links between each question and the possible answers. She also planned the rubric for the maze, including the response to incorrect answers.

The next stage was to create the maze in PowerPoint. This is the procedure she used to create the links between different slides:

1 To add a link to a button in PowerPoint, right-click on the button graphic and select *Hyperlink* or choose *Hyperlink* from the Insert menu.

2 Select *Hyperlink to* and in the drop-down menu choose *Slide …* then choose the slide you wish PowerPoint to jump to when the button is clicked (see Figure 5.5).

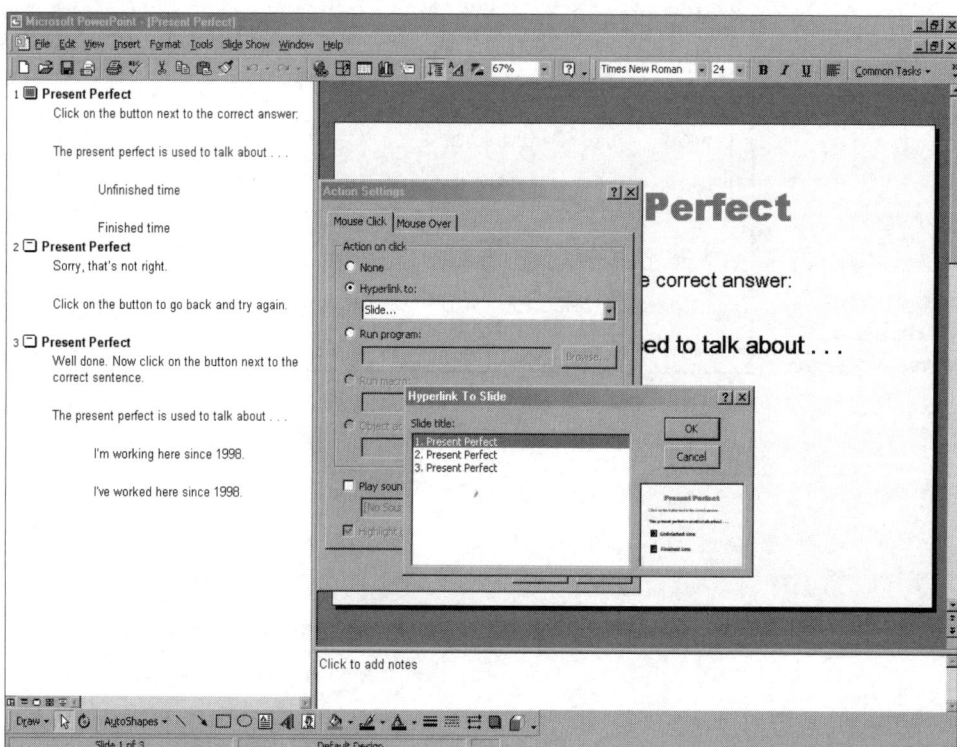

Figure 5.5
Making a link
in PowerPoint

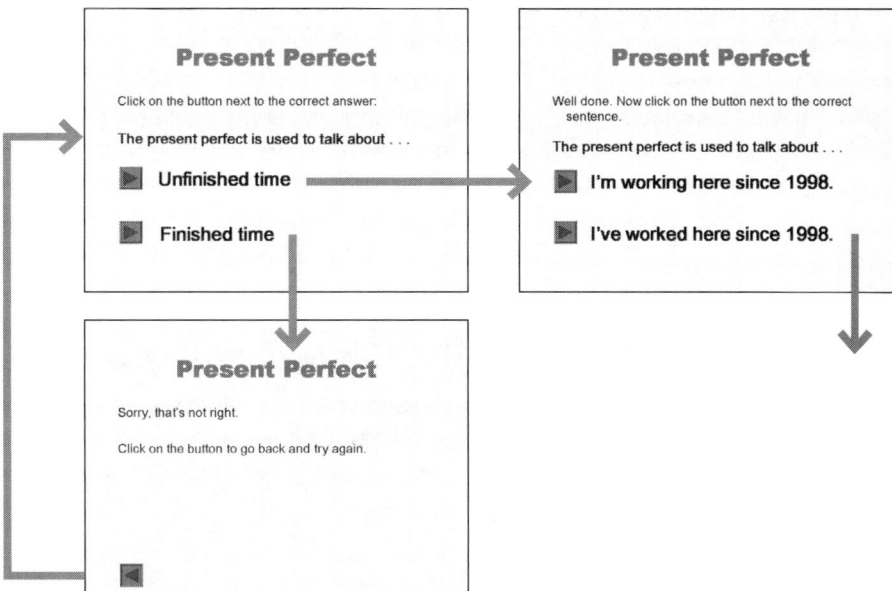

Figure 5.6
The start of the
Present Perfect
maze

When this first experiment was complete, the file size was less than 100Kb, so all of Ellen's learners were happy to have it emailed to them, which saved the expense of using CD-ROMs.

The maze was set as homework between classes. Before the next class, Ellen created a worksheet based on the content of the maze. At the end of the lesson, she asked her learners whether they felt they had completed the exercise more successfully as a result of having worked through the maze for homework or not. The responses fell into two groups: the first group felt it was too easy, while the second group felt they did not really understand why their answers where correct or not and said the maze was not able to answer their questions.

Ellen asked the class to vote on whether or not she should create further mazes on different topics. There was general support for a second experiment. For this second maze, Ellen focused on the language required for booking a hotel room on the phone. This allowed her to create a number of alternative narratives, depending on the choices of the learners. Choosing the appropriate responses resulted in successfully booking the type of room they wanted. Choosing inappropriate responses resulted in getting the wrong sort of room.

Again, the maze was set for homework, and, in the following lesson, the learners role-played the situation. This time, most members of the class agreed they had benefited from using the maze.

As a result of this second test, Ellen agreed to create more mazes based on functional language. However, as they became more complex, they took longer to create, so she promised to create a new one every couple of weeks. The learners retained each maze and used them as reviews.

Other teachers in the school started to use the mazes with their learners, and Ellen eventually gave a series of training sessions to show how she planned, created and used them.

This chapter will explore the features and benefits of using an interactive whiteboard (IWB). It will also look at some IWB software. Teachers who are able to teach using an interactive whiteboard are able to achieve a truly blended-learning solution – embedding technology such as the Internet, CD-ROMs, the Macmillan English Campus (see Chapter 3), PowerPoint (see Chapter 5), video and so on into their lessons in new and exciting ways.

How to use an interactive whiteboard

An IWB is a technology which essentially requires three things: a computer, an electronic projector and the interactive whiteboard itself. The most common configuration is where the computer is connected to the projector and whiteboard, and the projector displays the computer screen image on the whiteboard. Some whiteboards involve rear projection, where the projector is encased behind the IWB screen.

There are various types of IWB – some whiteboards have a hard surface, and some a soft surface. This surface is touch-sensitive. You can write on the surface with a special e-pen. Pens may come in different colours, such as red, green, blue and black. By tapping on the surface, you can control the computer in the same way as by using the computer mouse. When you write or draw on the whiteboard screen with the pen, any annotations you make can be saved as a new document. Note that with whiteboards that do not come with e-pens, you can interact with the board by using your finger.

There are a number of IWBs available on the market. Among the common producers of IWBs are SMART, Promethean and Cambridge-Hitachi. There are different sizes of IWB: one rule of thumb is 'the larger the classroom, the larger the IWB'. Each manufacturer produces a range of software.

An IWB allows you to run a range of normal computer programs in your language lesson. This could be office software such as Word, Excel and PowerPoint. It is also possible to use the Internet in the language classroom through an IWB, and this would therefore include other web-based products such as the Macmillan English Campus or the learners' Virtual Learning Environment (VLE). You can run videos or DVDs through the VLE, and, of course, CD-ROMs.

The software especially developed for IWBs may include maps, pictures and diagrams. In the SMART Board software, you can access these features by clicking on the 'Gallery' tab.

Much IWB software has been produced for content-based teaching within the state system. However, the amount of software available for ELT is growing. Coursebooks such as *Cambridge 365* (CUP) and *Cutting Edge* (Longman) now have accompanying software designed to be used on an IWB.

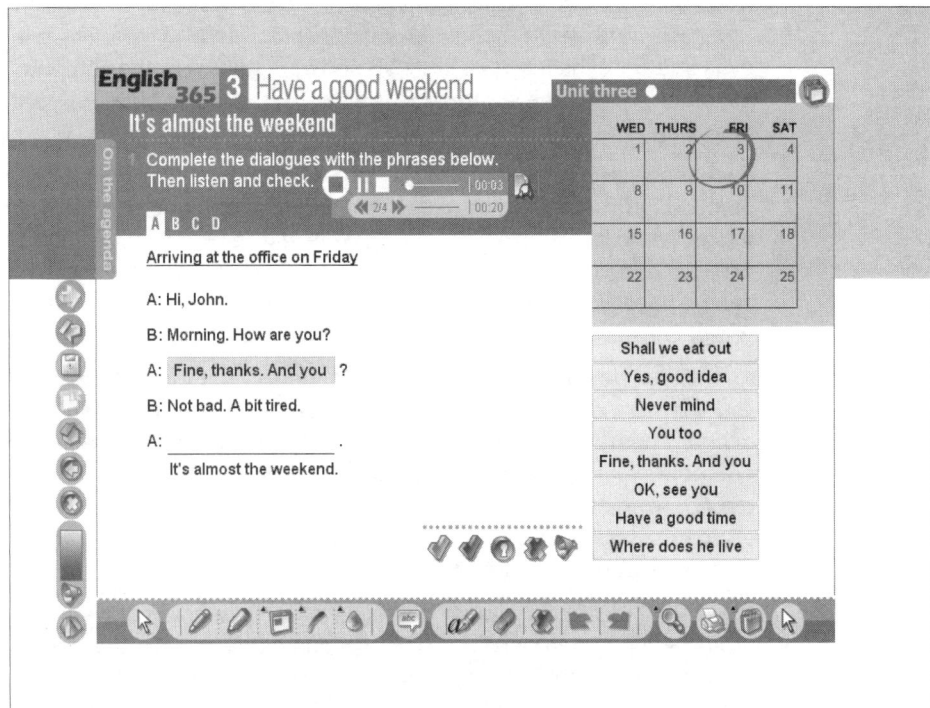

Figure 6.1
IWB software for
the Cambridge
365 course (CUP)

At the edge of the IWB is a toolbar containing a number of icons, many of which will be familiar or self-explanatory. The pen icon (or drawing tool) can be used for both drawing on screen and writing. Whatever you write on the IWB can be erased using the eraser tool. The highlighting tool can be used to highlight specific parts of a text. Handwritten script can be converted to text and saved as part of a document. This can be done by highlighting handwritten text and then tapping on the text-recognition tool. However, care must be taken when using the text-recognition tool. The software's ability to estimate what is on the board is only as accurate as the quality of the handwriting. This must be very clear. Long sentences should be avoided, because the software will read them as one object. If one word is misinterpreted, it cannot be highlighted and erased separately.

You can open a new document and write in text using the computer keyboard or a floating keyboard. The latter is an on-screen keyboard which allows learners to tap in letters and write text. These can be rather awkward to use, and the easiest way to incorporate longer texts is via the computer keyboard. You can also place hyperlinks into a document, click on these and go directly to a website.

Screens can be saved and reused in a future lesson. The sequence to do this is similar to other computer programs – click on 'Save as', give the document a name and save it into the relevant folder on the computer. A PowerPoint presentation projected onto the IWB can be annotated and the final product saved. A handout can be constructed by the group in class and then saved onto the college's files and distributed later.

In SMART Board, a special camera icon is used to take a screen shot of the IWB screen and save it. This enables you to use the original lesson fresh with another group, and also refer to the interesting notes made by previous groups which were captured in the screen shot.

Objects, including text and pictures, can be moved around on the IWB screen. This 'drag-and-drop' feature enables you to perform typical matching exercises. Pictures are available from the Internet, the IWB software gallery or the computer's hard drive. It is also possible to cover the screen and then uncover it bit by bit; this is sometimes known as 'masking'. The spotlight tool can be used to focus learners on one part of a picture.

Audio and video clips can also be played through the IWB using the on-screen controls. In some ELT software, the transcript of an audio clip can be shown on-screen. Sometimes, it is possible to highlight a section of this text using the highlighter tool, and the learners can listen to just this segment of the audio. When playing video clips to a class, the video can be paused and notes made on and around the images on the screen. Windows Media Player checks that you want to lose the notes before continuing with the screening.

An IWB can be combined with other technologies. By using a webcam, you can record your learners engaging in role-play activities and then replay the content to the learners to check mistakes. Voting devices, sometimes humorously referred to as 'voting eggs', are tools which allow learners to vote in class. In Promethean boards, this is known as the ACTIVote student response system. The results of the vote are displayed on-screen, often to dramatic effect. Learner voting can be anonymous, or you can view which way an individual learner has voted.

Using an IWB in a classroom is essentially an extension of good practice when using an ordinary whiteboard, so it is easy to become adept at using an IWB fairly quickly. The first time you use an IWB, it may still be slightly daunting. First, you need to follow a typical sequence for turning on the hardware. This involves turning on the computer and the electronic projector; the IWB will, in many configurations, automatically be turned on. It is advisable to arrive in the classroom early to check the equipment is working.

It is always advisable to have a training session before using an IWB. Such a session is usually run by the manufacturer, or there are some independent companies which organize training.

One development in the area of IWBs is mobility in the classroom. The use of an interactive wireless tablet means that you and your learners can control the digital content from different places in the room. Similarly, learners may control the board without coming out to the front. You or the learner writes or draws on the tablet, and the annotations can be seen on the IWB at the front of the room.

For more information on Interactive whiteboards, we suggest a site such as http://www.interactive-whiteboards.co.uk.

Opportunities and issues

An IWB can help make presentations dynamic, interesting and memorable for learners. Both you and your learners can prepare a PowerPoint presentation at home and bring it to class on a disk or saved on a memory stick.

An IWB is a perfect way to provide warmers, introductions to a topic, practice activities and so on. Even during a presentation, the learners can be involved, with you using some of the IWB tools, such as masking, to elicit answers from the learners. Learners can also come to the front of the class to demonstrate something or annotate the screen. An IWB can be used to promote group interaction and communication, too. However, using an IWB at certain key points in a lesson, can be more effective than using it continuously every lesson.

One key feature of an IWB is the facility to save any annotations which have been made during the lesson. The annotations may be made using the drawing tool, the highlighter or typed notes. You can then save the annotated page to the PC's hard drive. If you use the 'Save as' option, then the original lesson remains unaltered and can be used again with a future class. In a future lesson with a new group, you can show the saved notes as examples of the work of another group of learners.

The masking, or cover-up, feature can be used to great effect in a lesson. You can ask learners to predict the content of a lesson by revealing the picture bit by bit. In completing a language exercise, you can cover the questions and show only the answers. The learners then work in groups to construct the appropriate questions, providing practice in the tricky language area of question formation.

Using colour can be an effective way of re-enforcing a language point. In demonstrating word order in sentences, for example, verbs and nouns can be written in different colours. Text can have the same colour as the background, and is only revealed when the words are dragged onto a different part of the screen.

Figure 6.2 is an example of the use of masking combined with the use of colour. The learners, who are beginners, guess the names of the animals. By dragging the picture of the animal to the left, its name is revealed on the left of the screen. The text is the same colour as the screen, so it is hidden until moved. In this example, the picture of the dog has been dragged to the left, revealing the animal's name.

Figure 6.2
Use of masking and colour in an IWB

Having access to all of the normal computer files is one of the most exciting opportunities offered by IWBs. This can offer many chances for 'just-in-time' teaching. Should something crop up in a lesson which necessitates a visual, you can go to the Internet and use a search engine, then click on 'images' (see Chapter 2). Images can be downloaded in seconds that suit the background of your learners. Classes can be made culturally inclusive without having to scour through countless magazines and books. As a result, you have access to a large supply of pictures which may be saved on the computer's hard drive. The possibilities of incorporating the Web into a language lesson are exciting: learners can show their homepage or blog to other learners. Internet sites can be accessed quickly through typing a hyperlink onto the page. This saves the time spent in opening a web browser and locating a site through the favourites menu. Instead, one tap on the hyperlink brings up the site or relevant page immediately.

Voting eggs can be used to great effect in discussion lessons. In the middle of a debate, you can get an overview of how people are beginning to change their opinions. They can be used to check understanding: learners can vote on grammatical questions, and you can see whether a particular learner is weak in answering the questions. Learners can even use the device to tell you something – that they need help or they have finished an exercise.

One of the most important issues is cost. At the time of writing, the cost of an IWB is prohibitively high for many organizations. It is advisable to buy several IWBs for a institution, in order to maximize the chance that teachers will change their practice and start using them. Of course, the idea of buying several IWBs increases costs. In some parts of the world, their use is growing; for others, using an IWB is a distant dream.

Other issues concern classroom management. How to stand when using an IWB may need some practice. It is best to avoid standing in such a way as to cast a shadow over the screen, and it is important not to look directly into the electronic projector. Writing on-screen with an e-pen also takes a bit of getting used to. It may seem that as you write, the actual words appear slightly lower down on the screen. This can be disorientating. It indicates that the whiteboard needs to be recalibrated, a process to align the screen which involves tapping at certain points on the surface. It is usually necessary to recalibrate an IWB every month or so.

Finally, it is a good idea to be in the classroom early in order to check through the technology. No technology is infallible. There are times when there will be a glitch. If you intend to use an IWB, you do need to have a back-up plan worked out in case there are technical problems.

Practical activities

Where are you from?

Aim: to raise awareness of where classmates' home towns are

Level: beginner/elementary

Interaction: individual and group

Rationale: Learners are often unable to catch the names of their classmates' hometowns in a multi-lingual class; use of maps can bring the process of getting to know each other alive.

Technology: IWB / map-of-the-world software

Before class: Copy the map of the world in the software package onto the first page of the whiteboard notebook.

Procedure:

1 Learners interview each other to find out about each others' family and hometown.

2 Before the reporting stage, bring up the world map, or continent map as appropriate. Each learner reports back on his/her classmate. After they mention their hometown, ask the interviewee to go to the front of the class and mark their hometown on the map. Learners can write their initials or names next to the town.

3 At the end of the activity, save the map as a document on the hard drive in your folder. It is possible to print this off later and copy it for the class.

Variations: It is easy to develop this idea so that learners can research about their hometowns and present a picture presentation using PowerPoint.

Comparatives and superlatives

Acknowledgement for this idea: Francis Jones

Aim: to reinforce comparatives and superlatives

Level: elementary

Interaction: Learners come out to the front of the class to use the IWB.

Rationale: This activity shows how colour can be used effectively. Colour is appreciated by visual learners, and used to great effect to make patterns memorable. In this case, the learners can see the words (*small, beautiful, clean,* etc) but not the answers.

Technology: IWB

Before class: Prepare a list of appropriate adjectives using purple text. Write their comparatives and superlatives below in yellow (see Figure 6.3).

Procedure:

1 Ask learners to tell you the comparative and superlative forms of the adjectives on the IWB.

2 To reveal the answers, drag the word over to the right-hand side. Learners can check their guesses. You may also wish to ask learners to come up to the board and drag a word across themselves, after they have told the class what they think the right answer is.

Variations: If there are around 20 examples on the screen, you may wish to ask individual learners for the answer to one example and drag the word across yourself.

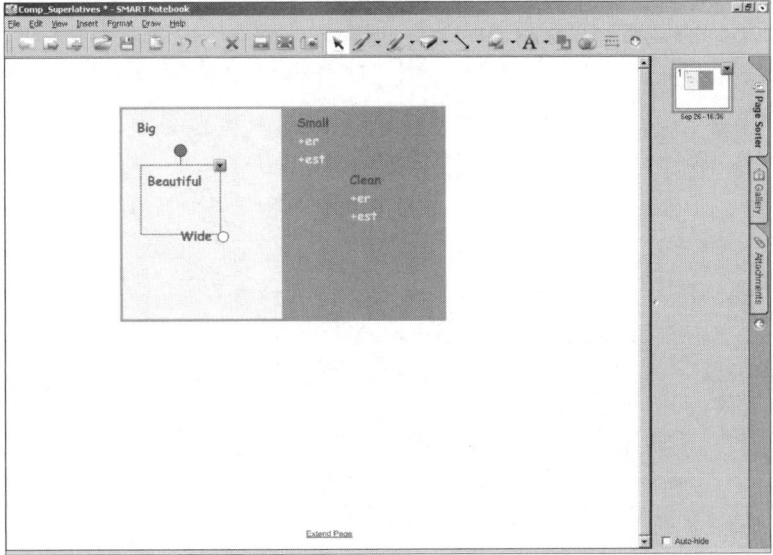

*Figure 6.3
Comparatives
and superlatives*

Preposition practice

Acknowledgement for this idea: Francis Jones

Aim: to practise prepositions

Level: elementary

Interaction: individual or pairs / learners come out to the front

Rationale: This activity also shows how colour can be used effectively in the class.

Technology: IWB

Before class: You should have the material (see Figure 6.4) saved.

Procedure:

1 Tell learners they are reviewing prepositions of place. Drag down the box on the left-hand side to reveal prepositions of place one by one.

2 Ask a learner to come up to the board and place the black ball in the right place in relation to the square on the right.

3 Move on to the second page. This is the same exercise done the other way round, ie learners drag the descriptions across to match the pictures.

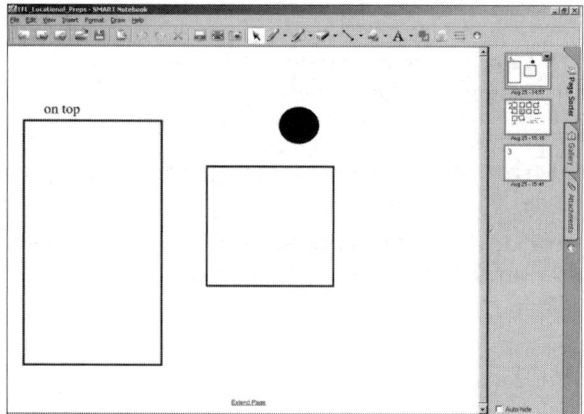 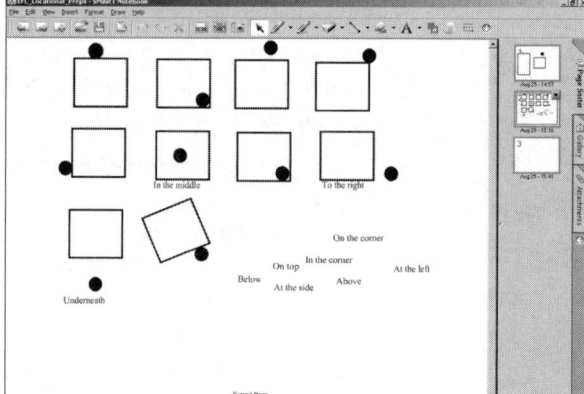

Figure 6.4 Prepositions of place

Case study

Case study: Introducing interactive whiteboards into a language school

A language school in Asia was keen to introduce IWBs. This was partly to keep up with the expectations of their learners, some of whom would assume that a school should be equipped with state-of-the-art technology. The Director of Studies issued a questionnaire to the teachers as to how they felt about the idea of buying IWBs for each classroom. Many expressed a number of concerns, such as 'What happens if it goes wrong?' and 'Will we still be able to use the old whiteboards?'. The school management decided to proceed regardless, removed all the old whiteboards and installed an IWB into each classroom. They choose SMART Boards. The teachers received a training course on how to use the new IWBs. The trainer ran through basic practices, such as the initial aligning of the whiteboard with the projector.

The teachers were quite concerned that they would not be able to proceed with their lesson plan if there was a technical problem. In fact, the technology proved quite reliable. A questionnaire some months later revealed that none of the teachers wished to return to using the old whiteboards, despite their original fears. In a teacher-training session, the Director of Studies asked the teachers to share some of their experiences. One teacher said that when one of her learners left the course, the group worked together in-class to write him an email, which was sent during the lesson. This was motivating and enjoyable for the learners. Another said that she was able to do a lesson on the future by getting learners to check their predictions for the weather against the forecast on the BBC website. The teachers were very enthusiastic about the IWBs and were able to see more potential in using them than had been tapped into so far. However, there was general agreement that the old whiteboards should not have been taken out, and strong agreement that they should be put back on a different wall, as a back-up, to stick up coursework produced by the learners and to be used alongside the IWB. Reservations were expressed about the effectiveness of the handwriting conversion tool, which was not seen as particularly reliable.

A portable device is anything you can carry around and can run on a battery. This includes personal digital music players, mobile phones, Personal Digital Assistants, or PDAs (small handheld or palm computers), laptops, digital audio recorders and dictaphones, digital cameras and digital camcorders. These devices can be used either to play digital media – photographs, audio or video – or to create it. Used appropriately, they can provide learners with opportunities for further language practice outside the classroom.

Using portable devices

Some of these devices serve the same purpose as the equipment we have been familiar with in classrooms for many years: the cassette recorder and video camera. The sound and images are stored in digital formats, which can be replayed and reviewed using the device which captured them or transferred to a computer. They can then be stored, edited, modified, incorporated into other computer documents, or compressed and passed to other people using email, CD-ROM or DVD.

Digital recording devices are much smaller than their older analogue equivalents and increasingly use on-board memory. Although this means you do not need tapes, some devices, such as digital cameras, are sold with only a small amount of memory. In order to store more photographs, you will need to buy a memory card with a greater capacity, but the prices of these are falling all the time.

Most recording devices can be set to an automatic mode, making them very easy to use. Many also offer other modes which give more advanced users greater control over how the device operates.

Digital content can be transferred, for example, from camera to computer, with no loss of sound or picture quality. Audio, photographs and video can be converted to different digital file formats to be played on devices such as music players or mobile phones.

Mobile phones and PDAs

These devices have acquired more and more features. Mobile phones can often take photographs or video clips. Although the image quality is lower than a dedicated piece of photographic equipment, they can be used for some of the ideas proposed in the 'Practical applications' section of this chapter. Many models of both devices are capable of storing and playing mp3 audio files through headphones.

Digital audio recorders

There are three different portable devices which can be used to make digital audio recordings: digital dictaphones, mp3 players and laptop computers.

Digital dictaphones

Digital dictaphones are very small and light, have built-in microphones and speakers, run on batteries and can store many hours of audio. They can be connected to a computer to transfer the audio files. They normally come packaged with software which, when installed on your computer, makes the transfer and handling of audio files straightforward. They often have a socket for connecting an external microphone for better sound quality. They also have a headphone or line-out socket so that the device can be connected in the traditional way to an external amplifier and then to speakers, which overcomes the problems of using the tiny, built-in speaker. This can be a useful alternative to transferring the files to a computer to be played. A final technical advantage of digital dictaphones is storage. Even the most basic models can store several hours of continuous audio or dozens of individual recordings.

Mp3 players

Some mp3 players designed for music also have a built-in microphone which allows you to record sounds from your environment. The drawback with these devices is that the microphone is very small and the quality of the recording correspondingly reduced. They also lack speakers, so you have to transfer the sound file to a computer if more than one person at a time wants to hear the playback.

Laptop computers

All computers have an input for a microphone, and some laptop computers have built-in microphones. You need audio-recording software if you want to use the computer directly as the recording device. This set-up is less mobile than the two portable devices explained above.

Many computers come with some sort of audio-recording software pre-installed. If yours does not, or you find this software unsuitable, try Audacity which is a free piece of software. You can use it to record and edit digital audio and to export the results as wav or mp3 files. To download Audacity, go to http://audacity.sourceforge.net. For more information on using Audacity, see *Podcasting* in Chapter 9.

Digital cameras

Digital cameras are principally designed to take photographs. These can then be printed in colour or black and white, or incorporated into word-processor documents or electronic documents such as web pages.

The quality of the photographic image your camera produces depends on the number of mega pixels it has. The higher the number, the better the image. However, this results in larger file sizes. If you want to add an image from a digital camera to a word-processor document or a web page, or if you want to email it, you should reduce the size first. This can be done using photo-manipulation software. There is a variety of such programs available. The most accessible will be the program that is included with your digital camera; however, there are a number of commercially available programs that give a range of different features, depending on price.

To change the size of a digital photograph, you first have to transfer it to a computer. This is done by connecting a lead between the camera and the computer or by removing the memory card of the camera and inserting it into a slot in the computer. You should consult the instructions of your individual camera for the correct procedure. Save the photograph in a logical folder (such as My Pictures on Windows computers or iPhoto on Macs). Start the photo-manipulation program, then use the Open command to open the photograph inside the program. Most programs of this type have a menu called Image which contains a command called Resize or Scale. Clicking on this gives you a range of choices, including the option to change the size of the image by changing its horizontal and vertical measurements in terms of pixels. A photograph straight from the camera will be measured in thousands of pixels. Changing this to hundreds will reduce the image size and the size of the resulting file.

This is a very general description of this process, and you will need to experiment with your camera and software. When you save the resized photograph, give it a new name. This allows you to retain the original image from the camera in case you want to use it again. Save the file using the jpeg file format. Not only is this the most flexible image format, but you can also select the degree to which the image file is further compressed. The higher the number, the larger the file and the better the image quality.

Digital camcorders

Digital camcorders record directly onto a DVD, which can then be played on a domestic DVD player or through a computer with a DVD drive. The very latest camcorders have mini hard drives, like a computer.

The video is transferred to a computer by connecting a lead between the two devices. The speed at which the data is transferred depends on the speed of your computer. The same applies if you want to edit digital video on your computer. Editing video requires a lot of processing power and can be beyond the capability of older computers. Always compare your computer's specifications with those required by the camcorder and the video-editing software.

Opportunities and issues

Using mobile phones and PDAs

The principal opportunity offered by many mobile phones and PDAs is the ability they share with music players to play digital audio files, which can be listened to through earphones. These files can be downloaded using a cable connected to a computer or, with some phones and PDAs, emailed as an attachment. This means that your learners can use devices that are part of their everyday lives and which they carry with them to school or work, or while traveling, to listen to recordings which can help them to improve their language skills.

These recordings could be those made in the classroom and which need to be reviewed for the purposes of feedback and correction. They could have been made by you to provide models of pronunciation. (See the 'Using digital recorders' section below for more information.) Alternatively, the recordings could be podcasts produced specially for language learners or authentic recordings from the thousands available on the Web. (See Chapters 2 and 3 for more information on podcasts.)

Using digital recorders

A digital recorder replaces the cassettes you used in the past. It can be used to record your learners during class either performing a drill such as pronunciation practice or engaging in free practice. You can then use the recording to highlight your learners' mistakes or to allow them to pick out things they got wrong. Outside the classroom, you can use a digital recorder to make recordings of your own voice for your learners. These can be pronunciation models of words or sounds that your learners need to practise and master, or longer recordings, such as dialogues, which model functional language. If your learners have access to this type of device, they can record themselves in order to practise pronunciation or as a homework exercise.

The compactness of such devices is a benefit. They are much easier to carry around for teachers who are on the move, and they are less obtrusive in the classroom, which can be an important factor if you have a learner who is nervous about being recorded.

The biggest opportunity presented by digital recorders becomes apparent when the audio files are transferred to a computer. They can be copied without any loss of sound quality and, like any other computer file, audio files can be given appropriate names, saved on networks, burned to CD-ROMs and DVDs or emailed. This means that recordings can easily be distributed to your learners, and, if you use a common file format such as mp3, they can be listened to using a variety of devices.

Using digital cameras

The most obvious opportunity offered by digital cameras is to take photographs which can be added to word-processor documents. You can use photographs of your learners to personalize materials. You can add photographs to a wide variety of teaching materials, such as vocabulary worksheets and grammar explanations. Photographs can be used as realia to initiate or stimulate classroom discussions. A digital camera allows you to acquire and print those photographs at very short notice or get images of places and things that you cannot bring into the classroom.

Your learners can also add photographs to documents they have produced. (See Chapter 5 for a practical application in which learners produce a class newspaper.)

Digital photographs can be added to electronic documents such as web pages. After a brainstorming lesson, it is a good idea to photograph the board in order to retain the information or vocabulary generated. This photograph can be posted onto a blog, or you could just keep it for your own reference in order to test the learners on the language at a later date.

Many digital cameras have tiny, built-in microphones. These can be used to record clips of audio which are attached to a photograph. This feature can be used by your learners to create simple audio-visual presentations.

Some digital cameras also offer the possibility to record video clips. However, since this is not what they were principally designed to do, the quality of both image and sound is rarely good enough for satisfactory recordings of what goes on in a language-learning classroom. If you want to be able to record moving images, it is better to invest in a digital camcorder.

Using digital camcorders

The uses for digital camcorders do not vary greatly from the uses of VHS video technology. Classes or presentations can be videoed, and the recording used to analyze the performance of your learners as part of the post-task feedback. Learners can use cameras to make their own short programmes based on scripts they have prepared, or interviews with each other or people inside and outside the school.

The significant benefit of digital technology is that the video can be edited using a desktop computer and a reasonably priced piece of software. The ability to edit introduces a number of possibilities. Programmes created by learners can be shot out of sequence and the best parts edited together; parts of a videoed fluency activity could be taken to demonstrate both the best language used and the areas that require the most work; and voice-overs, music and sound effects can be added.

Another advantage of using digital video is that it can be played back on computers, either using a built-in DVD player or from the hard drive. If the school where you work has a network, the video file can be stored on the server and viewed from computers around the network.

Practical activities

Pronunciation models

Aim: to provide pronunciation models

Level: elementary to advanced

Interaction: whole class then individual

Technology: digital audio recorder and email

Rationale: You can create digital recordings of sounds and words to help with pronunciation. These can be made quickly and distributed to learners, who can listen whenever is convenient. It may even be possible to make recordings for individual learners in multi-lingual classes, depending on the time you have available to you.

Before class: During lessons, keep a note of words that your learners have problems with or regularly get wrong.

Procedure:

1 Write the words on the board and ask your learners to create sentences using these words. Drill them in saying these sentences.

2 After the lesson, use a digital dictaphone or other digital audio recorder to record the sentences yourself. Repeat each target word twice, followed by the sentence. Match your speed to the learners' level.

3 Transfer the audio file to a computer and, if necessary, convert it to mp3 format.

4 Email the file to each of your learners with instructions to listen to it as often as they wish before the next class.

5 In the next class, repeat the pronunciation drill.

Follow on: Make sure you recycle the words in question in other fluency activities.

Recorded presentations

Aim: to practise extended speaking outside class

Level: intermediate to advanced

Interaction: individual

Technology: digital audio recorder and email

Rationale: In this activity, the learner makes the recording and emails it to you. This works well with learners doing one-to-one courses. It is good for learners taking weekly classes, especially those who need to develop presentation skills.

Before class: If your learner does not have the technical skills to make and email the recordings, you will need to dedicate some time in earlier lessons to training them.

Procedure:

1 At the end of each lesson, agree on a topic for a short presentation. It could be directly related to the topic of the current lesson or something to be discussed in the next lesson.

2 Between lessons, your learner prepares a five- to ten-minute presentation on the agreed topic, records it using a digital audio recorder, then emails the file to you.

3 You listen to the file and prepare comments and language feedback.

4 At the next lesson, you and your learner examine the feedback and, if there is time, the learner repeats the presentation, incorporating the changes.

Illustrated vocabulary exercises

Aim: to reinforce concrete vocabulary items

Level: beginner and elementary

Interaction: whole class

Technology: digital camera, word processor and printer

Rationale: Pictures are extremely helpful for lower-level learners learning vocabulary. With a digital camera, you can create worksheets with exercises that are illustrated by pictures from the learners' immediate environment or which focus on exactly the vocabulary they need.

Before class: Pre-teach the target language and use this activity as a review.

Procedure:

1 Use a digital camera to take photographs of concrete items of vocabulary your learners need.

2 Transfer the pictures to a computer. Then insert them into a word-processor program and create an exercise around the things shown in the pictures. See Figure 7.1 for an example.

3 You can use the worksheet as a test of your learners' knowledge or as a way of presenting the vocabulary.

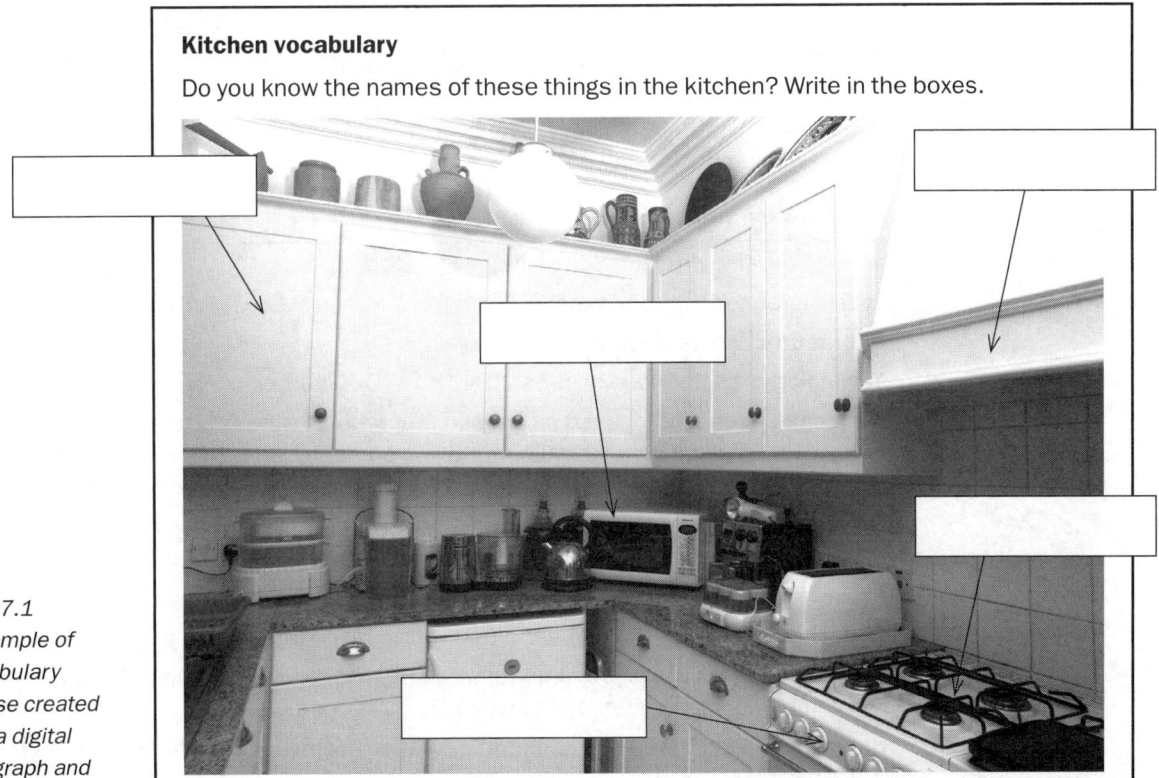

Figure 7.1
An example of a vocabulary exercise created using a digital photograph and a word processor

Photo and audio essays

Aim: to create a multimedia presentation

Level: intermediate to advanced

Interaction: pairwork or small groups

Technology: digital camera, computer with speakers and data projector (if available)

Rationale: Many digital cameras allow you to record short audio clips which are attached to a photograph. These can be combined to create simple audio-visual essays. This activity is attractive for young or teenage learners. It is also a reasonable substitute for using a camcorder.

Before class: A sample presentation or one from an earlier course can provide a useful model.

Procedure:

1 Explain the idea of using the digital camera and audio feature to create an essay, using an example if possible.

2 Suggest some possible subjects for such essays, for example, interviews with other learners and staff, or a study of the neighbourhood where they live. Find out whether your learners have any other suggestions.

3 Divide the class into pairs or small groups. Issue cameras and do any necessary technical training.

4 Tell the learners how long the essays should be, for example, ten pictures. Set a deadline for completion.

5 When the deadline arrives, transfer the image and audio files onto a computer.

6 Each pair or small group presents their essay, using the computer screen or a data projector.

Variation: An alternative is to create a single essay, with different pairs or small groups tasked with producing one part.

Presentation videos

Aim: to develop presentation skills

Level: intermediate to advanced

Interaction: whole class and individual

Technology: digital video camera, CD-ROM or DVD burner

Rationale: Presentations are a common feature of Business English courses and very often involve videoing the participants giving presentations. This allows analysis of not only the language and delivery, but also body language and the use of visuals.

Before class: Tell your learners they are going to prepare and give a presentation at an agreed future date. (See page 77 for a related activity.)

Procedure:

1 Each learner gives their presentation, which is recorded using a digital video camera.

2 The recordings of the presentations can then be viewed by connecting the camera to a computer or by transferring the video files to a computer.

3 Each learner can view his or her presentation in conjunction with any written feedback from you.

4 If this exercise is repeated later in the course, compare the latter presentation with the first one in order to identify areas of improvement, as well as areas for future study.

Follow on: At the end of the course, all of a learner's presentations can be burned onto a single DVD to take away with him or her.

Case study

A summer course project using digital camcorders

Nicholas had a class of teenage learners who were doing a four-week summer course. He decided to use digital camcorders to make a video document of the entire course. The target was to produce a DVD for the learners to take home which would contain video clips and any photographs taken during the course. In addition, it would contain written material, such as a class newspaper, vocabulary lists and learning advice written by him.

On the first day of the course, he explained the project to the class and introduced them to the two camcorders which he was planning to use. He told the learners that everyone would have an opportunity to be a camera operator during the course and that he would establish a rota to show who was going to video classes and presentations and who would be responsible for videoing the weekly outings. He also established a side project which required each of the class to prepare and video an interview with another person. Since they did not all know each other, he explained that this would not start until the second week of the course, when everyone could decide who they wanted to interview.

Initially, some of the class were reluctant to be videoed. Nicholas organized a fluency activity in small groups during which the camcorder was handed to a different person in the class every five minutes. They could video what they liked, but must respect the wishes of those who did not want to appear. This activity was very popular, and afterwards the class watched the results. Once they had seen this video, those who were initially not keen to take part agreed to try.

As the course progressed, everybody got their turn to be camera operator. Inevitably, some people were better at it than others, and so some of the video recordings were unusable. One of the problems that came up was the quality of the sound from the camcorder's microphone. The classroom had a high ceiling, and this resulted in an echoey sound. Nicholas found that a microphone placed on a table in the centre of the room closer to the learners achieved better sound quality. It also meant the camera operator could no longer move around, so the camcorder was placed on a tripod for classroom videos, which resulted in steadier images.

The video produced on the outings was the most interesting for the learners. Nicholas divided them into four groups and made each one responsible for the editing of the video from each trip, and preparing and recording a voiceover for that video. Again, the results were variable, but many learners reported that it was one of activities they enjoyed most on the course.

The peer interviews also varied in terms of quality and how seriously the participants took the activity. However, the learners who prepared well and understood its purpose as a language exercise produced excellent results.

At the end of the course, Nicholas asked the class to decide which clips they thought should go on the DVD. Members of the class made their nominations, and the class voted on which should be included. Finally, Nicholas selected as many of these as would fit on the DVD and burned a copy for each learner in time for the last day of the course.

Computer-mediated communication, or CMC, refers to situations as diverse as communicating through the keyboard with penpals overseas, sending an email across the world, or making a telephone call across the Internet, using a system such as Skype™. This chapter looks at the range of ways in which learners and teachers can communicate through the medium of the computer – chat, email, forums and video-conferencing – and then describes the use of a Virtual Learning Environment (VLE) in language teaching.

CMC can be divided into 'synchronous' and 'asynchronous' communication. Synchronous communication refers to communication which takes place in real time, such as chat. An ordinary telephone call is also synchronous. Asynchronous communication refers to communication which takes place at different times. Sending an email and replying to it is asynchronous.

There are a number of ways in which CMC can play a role in structured language study. At the extreme, learners taking an entirely online course with a so-called 'virtual school', such as Englishtown or Global English, will be using CMC. Elsewhere, learners may take a course partially online. These courses are sometimes called hybrid courses or POLL (partially online language learning). It is also common to use the term *blended learning* to describe such a course.

CMC might also be used in other teaching scenarios. For example, imagine you teach a group and see them once a week. You know your learners have email addresses, and so you decide to communicate with your learners outside of the normal class hours. They start to email their homework tasks to you as assignments. Or imagine the following: you work at a university which uses a Virtual Learning Environment such as Blackboard. When you meet your learners, you issue their Blackboard access address and password, which means learners can log on to the VLE. As the course develops, you begin to develop online materials and post the handouts on the VLE. Your learners take timed tests and submit their assignments on the VLE.

As these examples and varieties demonstrate, the possible applications of CMC are extremely diverse.

Forms of computer-mediated communication

Text chat

Text chat is a synchronous form of communication involving, exactly as the term suggests, people communicating through writing to each other, using their computer keyboard as the mode of input. There are a number of different types of text chat. It is possible to chat with one person online, or several. One of the commonest types of text chat is chatting to others in a chat room – a virtual space where users can read on-screen messages.

Your learners may well be already using text-based CMC and communicating in English with friends across the world as part of their everyday lives. You can incorporate similar activities in your classes and have your learners communicate with other learners around the world.

The first thing you need to do is set up chat by choosing a program such as MSN Messenger. This is quite easy, as all you need to do is follow the online instructions. Visit: http://webmessenger.msn.com.

The first step after signing up is to add people to your address book. You will also need to know that your learners have accounts, and if these are compatible. MSN and Yahoo! are now compatible. When you are using your computer, the MSN programme runs in the background. You can see which of your contacts is online. To send them a message, simply type in the text box at the bottom of the MSN window and hit enter. If several people are connected to the session, they will all see the same message, so you can chat to several contacts online at the same time. Internet users can log on to one of the many chat rooms and join in one of the many topics being discussed with participants from all over the world.

During a chat session, there are a number of things to notice. There is a slight time lag which occurs between someone typing a message and the time it appears on your screen. You may be replying to a previous message when the next message appears. The time lag in sending messages across the Internet is less noticeable as Internet connection speeds increase. Nevertheless, because of this delay and the fact that many people are posting messages at the same time, users may experience a sense of communication being 'disjointed', as messages may appear onscreen slightly out of sync. Communication in chat, if you are chatting with more than one person, may be bewildering to newcomers. Also, regular users use slang expressions and abbreviations.

Most beginners spend a period of time 'lurking' – that is, just watching what is going on without necessarily making a contribution. Anonymity and the use of nicknames are a feature of using chat forums. It is possible to have a private conversation with one person involved in the communication (known as 'whispering'). Text-based communication includes many of the features of speech (unfinished sentences), but is actually practising the skill of writing.

There are other chatting systems which are worth considering. IRC stands for Internet Relay Chat. This is a virtual meeting place. It is possible to participate in group discussions on one of the thousands of IRC 'channels' – the name for a discussion forum. You can also just talk in private to family or friends. IRC was originally designed for group communication.

A word of warning: open chats on the Internet are frequently used for undesirable conversations; most learners will of course be 'net savvy' and aware of these dangers. Nevertheless, you might want to avoid such problems by using 'closed' chat sessions.

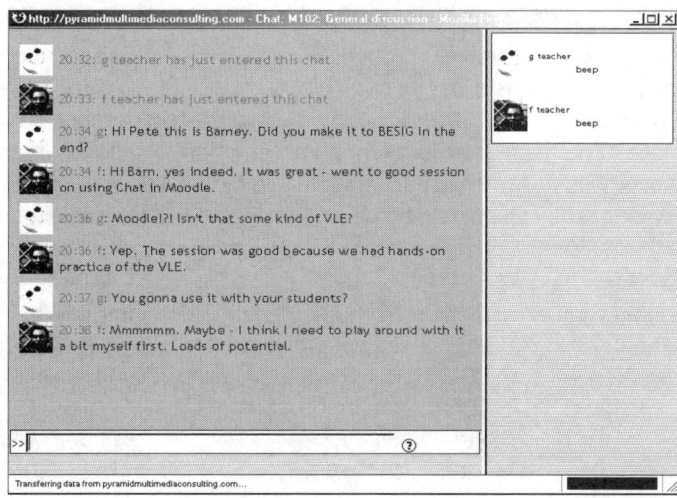

Figure 8.1
Sample of
dialogue in
a chat room

MOOs

MOOs are another environment on the Internet that can be used for chatting. MOO is usually taken to stand for Multi-Object Orientation. This is a virtual environment which allows more than one person at a time to chat. In order to explore a MOO, we suggest visiting: http://schmooze.hunter.cuny.edu. This is probably the most well-known MOO in ELT. It was established in 1994 as a place where people studying English as a foreign language could practise English and share ideas with other learners. Learners have opportunities for one-on-one and group conversations. They can access language games such as Scrabble, a virtual library and a grammar maze. Working in MOOs may appeal to more imaginative types, since all the communication takes place through text only.

If you wish to use chat with your learners, there are a number of options available. You could use a MOO environment, either text-based – eg SchMOOze – or with two-dimensional graphics, such as Tapped In (http://tappedin.org/tappedin) or The Palace (http://www.thepalace.com). Alternatively, you can use a private chat room which you can upload to your website. If you wish to do this, try using spinchat (http://www.spinchat.com). If you do not have your own space on the Web, make a chat room available. An example of such a chat room is found at Chatshack (http://chatshack.net).

Email

Email stands for electronic mail. The sending and receiving of emails pre-dates the Web and has now become ubiquitous. It is not an exaggeration to say that most teachers have an email account, and most learners too.

As part of connecting a computer to the Internet, you will also be guided to set up an email account which you can manage through a program such as Outlook Express, which is part of Windows, or Safari on a Mac. If you do not have a computer, you can set up a free, web-based account. Visit http://www.hotmail.com or http://www.yahoo.com and follow the instructions.

It is possible to send an email to one person or many. You can also send attachments in a range of file formats, usually by clicking on the *Attach (files)* button and selecting a file from your computer's hard drive. It is worth remembering that large files may take a long time to download on a slow connection, and that some people's anti-spam software may be set to block files over a certain size. You can find out the file size of a document by going to My computer, right-clicking on the file icon and then clicking on 'Properties'.

It is not always easy to convey emotions in the sending of emails, such as whether what you are typing is intended as a joke or not. This has given rise to the emergence of 'smileys' and 'emoticons'. 'Smiley' is derived from the fact that the symbol, on its side, looks like a smiling face. 'Emoticon' is a word formed by 'emotion' and 'icon'. In addition, the rise in the sending of emails has been in part responsible for the rise in the number of abbreviations used in writing, such as *atb* (all the best). See Figure 8.2 for a selection of these.

Figure 8.2
Examples of emoticons, abbreviations and useful email terms

Emoticons		Abbreviations		Useful terms
:-)	smiley face	BTW	by the way	netiquette – Internet etiquette
:-D	laugh	FYI	for your information	(eg don't capitalize, because
;-)	wink	LOL	laugh out loud	it looks like shouting)
:-(	sad face	OTOH	on the other hand	
		atb	all the best	to flame – to fire off an email
		thnx	thanks	when angry

Emails have been described as 'talky-writing' because they contain elements of both speech and writing.

Forums and bulletin boards

A common form of online communication is to leave a message for others in a forum, such as a Yahoo! Group. Participants who join such a forum clearly have a common interest. Joining a forum is easy; visit a site such as http://www.yahoo.com.

Another example of a place where users can leave messages is the BBC website, where you can read an article and post your reactions and comments.

A bulletin board is an electronic version of a noticeboard. Here, a user can leave a message for anyone to read. Also, a user can review a message left by someone else and all messages posted can be read by every user. A computerised bulletin board is commonly known as a BBS. This is essentially the same as a forum. Users wishing to contribute can follow what is known as a thread – one particular theme or discussion which is being debated.

It is now possible to leave voice messages on a bulletin board. You may use a system such as the Wimba audio bulletin board, which can be used inside a VLE such as Blackboard (see Figure 8.3).

Figure 8.3
The type of exchanges possible with an audio bulletin board. This one is Wimba audio bulletin board, which can be used in Blackboard.

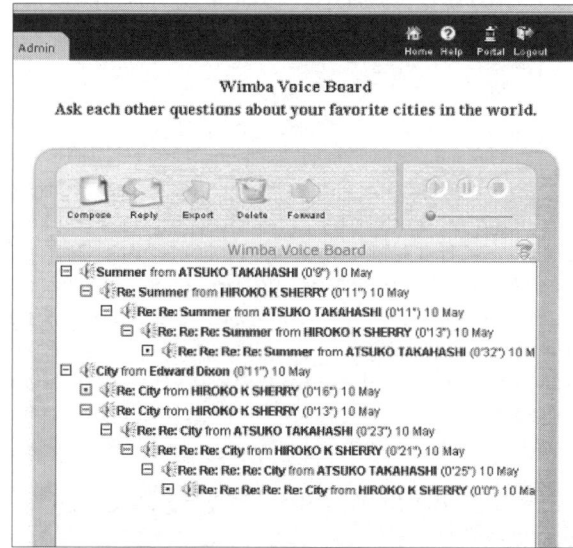

Video-conferencing

Video-conferencing allows people to communicate in real time with others via a video and audio link. Video-conferencing is a form of communication which occurs frequently in the business world. There are a number of different types of video-conferencing. At the more sophisticated end of the spectrum is satellite video-conferencing, where the technology is provided by a telecommunications company. At the other end is the use of a desktop video camera linked to a computer and used between two people who can see each other on their computer screen.

At a conference, one session may involve the live broadcast of an event, such as a plenary session, to an audience watching the transmission remotely in another venue. Another common set-up is a group conference involving people communicating from several different venues. Everyone logs in to the conference from their own location. Two classes can communicate using video-conferencing. The type of video-conferencing which is of most interest here is the type which links person to person, teacher and learner: two computers connect to each other across the Internet, using a desktop video camera and software such as CU-See me. The speakers use a headset and a microphone. Now that high-speed Internet connectivity is more widely available at a reasonable cost, this type of desktop video-conferencing is now accessible to many, and has become a popular option in Internet cafés.

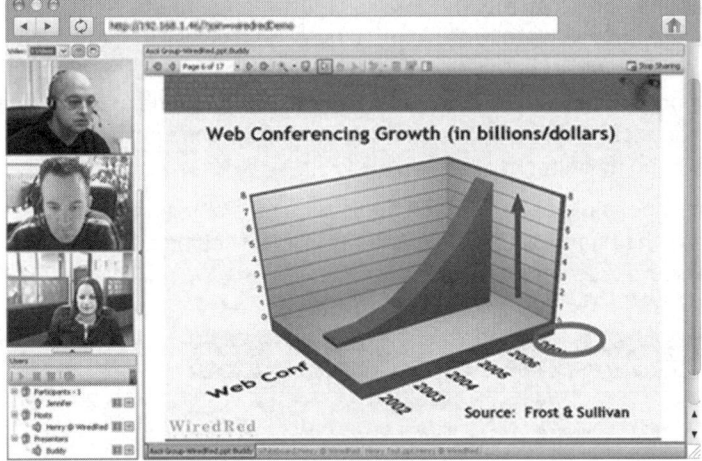

Figure 8.4
Three people
involved in a
video-conference,
with one of the
speakers showing
a presentation

Setting up the facilities for a desktop video conference is surprisingly cheap and easy. You need to buy a video camera (webcam) for both computers and attach it to the screen. Many laptop computers today already have a built-in camera. Both parties should then load the necessary software. Microsoft Netmeeting is one way of communicating remotely and runs with a desktop video camera. You can prepare a class using the 'shared whiteboard' function. This involves you writing your tasks on pages in the whiteboard and saving them for the lesson. A shared whiteboard lets a group of people communicate by typing comments, drawing, highlighting and pointing, and is also a feature within a VLE (see Figure 8.5).

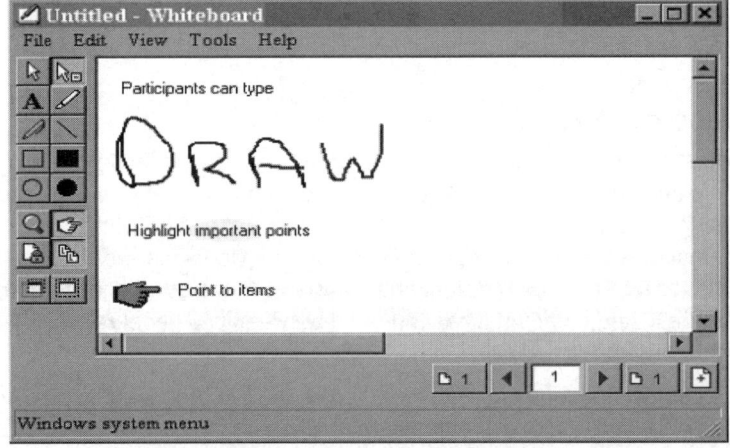

Figure 8.5
Shared whiteboard
feature within
Microsoft's
Netmeeting

Try CU-See Me for free video chat and virtual chat space. For more information on this option, visit: http://commtechlab.msu.edu/sites/Letsnet/noframes/bigideas/b9/b9u3l2.html.

For more on desktop video-conferencing, we recommend reading the chapter 'Using Internet-based audio-graphic and video-conferencing for language teaching and learning' (Regine Hampel and Eric Baber) in *Language Learning Online: Towards Best Practice* (ed. Uschi Felix, 2003).

Audio-conferencing

Telephone audio-conferencing has been available for many years. A more recent development of interest to language teachers and learners is the rise in VoIP. VoIP stands for Voice over Internet Protocol. Skype™ is one well-known example of a system enabling telephone calls to be made over the Internet. Skype™ is a peer-to-peer Internet telephony network. It includes free and pay-for services. Among its many features are both voice- and video-conferencing. Skype™ competes with other VoIP services. Signing up is relatively straightforward. First, you need to visit the Skype™ site at http://www.skype.com. After downloading and installing the free software, you need to choose a user name and password, then add people to your Skype™ address book. The process is similar to that of registering for MSN Messenger.

Virtual Learning Environments (VLEs)

A virtual learning environment is a web-based platform designed to support teachers in the management of online educational courses. A VLE consists of 'communication tools', such as email and a discussion board, and tools for organizing the administration of a course. A further dimension involves the testing of learners, through quizzes, and the dissemination of information. A VLE is sometimes referred to as an LMS (Learning Management System) or a CMS (Course Management System).

A VLE is essentially empty, in the sense that it has no content until material is created to populate it. This material could be provided by teachers; they can upload Word documents and PowerPoint presentations to the site, create online quizzes or import streaming video or audio files. Alternatively, the institution may buy publisher-created digital content. Such materials may be customizable to a specific course.

VLEs are often used by universities, and a learning technologist is usually employed to deal with the technical issues such as the uploading of materials. Blackboard and Moodle are two of the best-known VLEs, both commonly used in universities (see Figure 8.8). One important difference is cost – an institution pays a comparatively high cost to use or lease Blackboard, whereas the actual Moodle software is free. There is a charge to host a Moodle site.

With Blackboard, it is possible to experiment with the platform by creating materials and have them hosted on the site free for a period of time, after which you need to pay a fee. This allows you to become familiar with the platform. Moodle is a CMS which uses an Open Source software package designed on pedagogical principles. It aims to help educators create effective online learning communities, with emphasis on the concept of 'community'. You can download and use it on any computer. It is relatively easy to install on a PC to test it and develop courses offline. The Open University in the UK has adopted it as their platform. Moodle is a comprehensive platform and can support many types of database (particularly MySQL). For more information, see http://www.blackboard.com, http://moodle.org and http://download.moodle.org/docs/teacher-manual.pdf for Moodle.

At its simplest, a VLE is a delivery system for documents and other information, and in many higher-education environments, this is how it is used. Instead of having to deal with paper print-outs, learners can pick up material, deliver exercises and find out information about the course electronically on the VLE. This requires little more technical knowledge than sending an attachment using web mail. At the other end of the spectrum, it is possible to develop quite sophisticated courses, involving automatically marked placement tests, group projects using synchronous and asynchronous communication, webquests and many other methods applicable to a blended-learning environment. All this can be done with no programming knowledge.

At the homepage of the VLE, you will type in your user name or staff ID, and then your password. This will take you to the VLE entry page (see Figure 8.6).

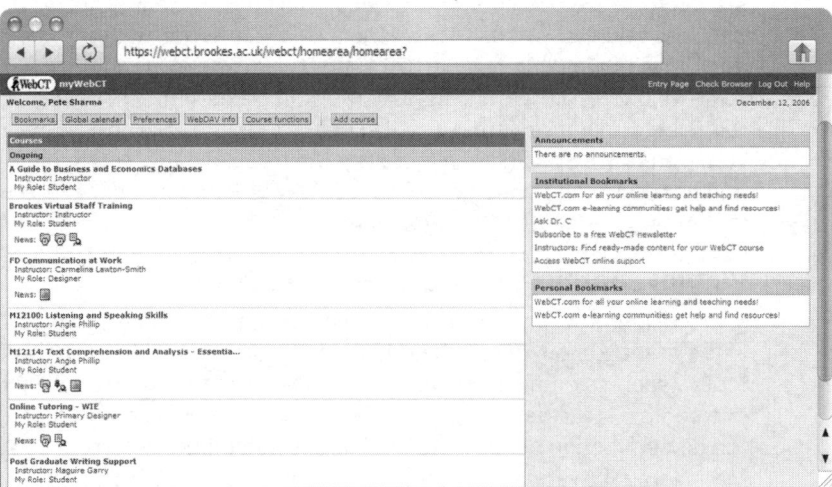

Figure 8.6
VLE entry page

This entry page displays all of the courses you are running. If you click on a course title, you will go to the course homepage (see Figure 8.7).

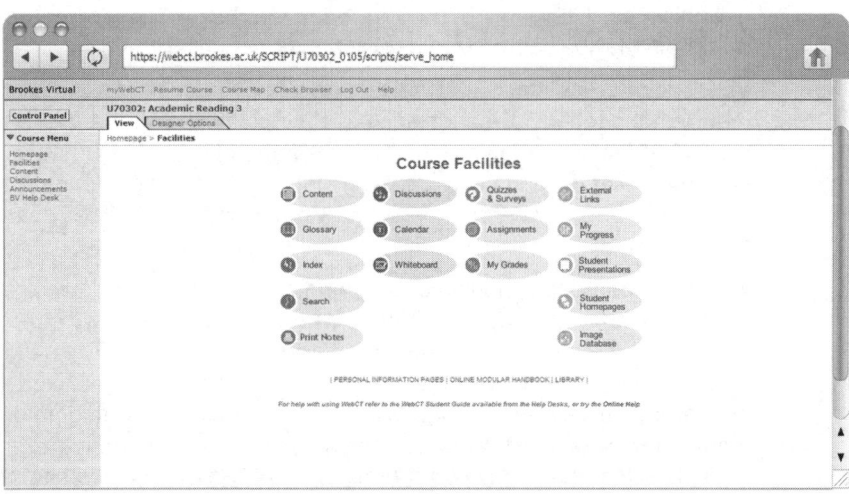

Figure 8.7
Course homepage

From here, both the teacher and learners can then access the week-by-week contents page of the course (see Figure 8.8), and access any material for each class.

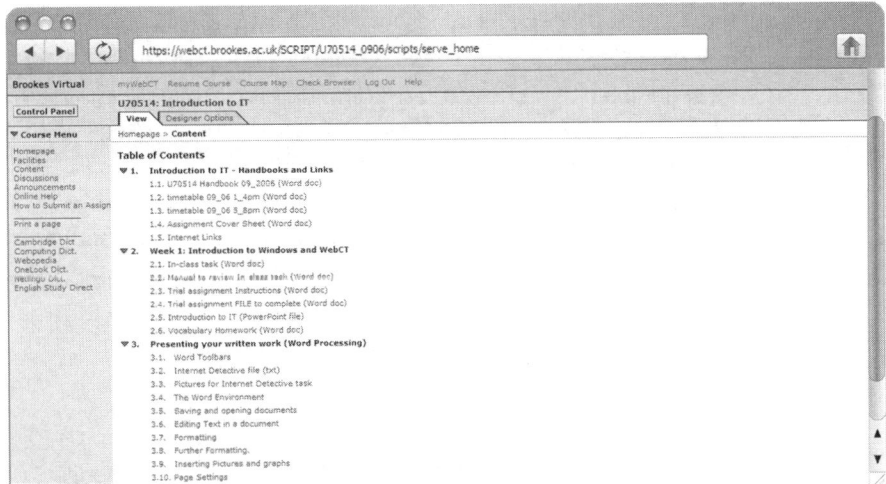

Figure 8.8
Course outline

It is possible to log in at a higher level as a course designer. This involves the creation of content. Course content includes what are commonly referred to as learning objects. A learning object is usually defined as a self-contained piece of learning material with an associated learning objective, which could be of any size and in a range of media. Learning objects are capable of reuse by being combined together with other objects for different learning purposes. Generally, learning objects within a VLE should fulfil a specific aim, and they should be designed to be reusable.

It is recommendable to take a course to become familiar with course creation tools. These are not as daunting to use as you may imagine, and some are quite intuitive. With a little effort, you can upload learners' recorded presentations onto the VLE, or allow the learners themselves to upload material. There is great scope for the imaginative development of courses using a VLE.

Opportunities and issues

CMC can benefit language learning in a number of ways. It can promote reflection and noticing of features of language. It can involve collaboration and involve the 'scaffolding' of learning, as learners work together to achieve a task and support each other.

Synchronous CMC can help develop fluency, with learners having to react and communicate in real time, concentrating on fluency. Asynchronous CMC can help develop deeper thinking skills, with time for writers to consider accuracy, develop an argument, and rewrite their contribution.

One of the biggest opportunities afforded by communication across the Internet is to open the world of the classroom and enable learners to communicate with learners in another country, maybe as part of a project.

Using text chat

Chat may well offer learners a chance to develop their language abilities. For instance, they are using the keyboard in real time, and concentrating on fluency and communication. When text chat conversation partners do not understand what a learner has written, they will tell them, forcing the writer to rephrase his or her message. This 'negotiating of meaning' can arguably work towards improving your learners' language abilities. However, if there is no teacher, it is quite likely that learners will continue to replicate their mistakes or not take advantage of the learning opportunities provided by the activity.

One of the main benefits offered by chatting is the fact that some learners who are normally shy in a face-to-face class may actually become less shy and express themselves in a different way through a different medium.

The use of chat outside the classroom may help to make the group gel together, and could have a socially cohesive purpose. You can offer to be in a chat forum at a certain time. Anyone in the class who wishes to log on and communicate can do so.

It is possible to print out the complete chat conversation. This gives you the chance to analyze learner input and give feedback accordingly.

Using email

Email offers many opportunities for language teachers and learners. You can encourage learners to email another class. The ePALS Classroom Exchange® maintains a community of collaborative classrooms engaged in cross-cultural exchanges, project sharing and language learning. Visit the e-pals website on http://www.epals.com.

You and your learners can be in regular communication between face-to-face classes. Email allows for an authentic purpose for writing, such as reorganizing the time for a class. The most obvious examples are to mail learners with a pre-lesson task, and to send and receive homework tasks.

The fact that electronic text can be copied and pasted, and easily edited, means that it is an ideal medium in which to give language feedback. Your responses can be threaded through the original text, which can then be mailed back to the learner. Another opportunity is the chance to give colour-coded correction. By changing the colour of the text in a reply, it is easy for a learner to identify the comments. Language corrections could be made in red, and other comments in blue. You can also use features such as Word's 'Track changes' or 'Insert comment' (see page 73).

In an email exchange, there is a record of the previous messages. This can be printed out and used for language analysis. Learners can be encouraged to reflect on their output.

The networked computers in a language school will most likely have email, and sending an email from one computer to another is more or less instantaneous. It is possible to capitalize on this feature of a network. You can set up a role-play, using prompt cards, with individual learners. This is a good medium to send your learners a real-world message, eg about a change of classroom or a message such as 'The social programme on Thursday has been cancelled. Do you have any suggestions?'. Bearing in mind their work, you could invent a situation such as 'I am visiting [your home town] next month. Pls could you advise on places to visit. Thnx.'

Use the ideas on telephone role-play cards in your school and adapt them for emails.

Another opportunity is afforded by listening to your learners as they work together composing an email. Monitoring the discussion can give you insights into task process, while learners are concentrating on creating the product. Typically, learners may be unaware of the negative impact of their email, as are some native speakers. This aspect of sending an email is a good area to focus on when you give feedback.

If your learners need to write emails, but you do not have the facility, you could try using a blank email form (see page 146). Photocopy this and have learners write to someone else in the class and 'send' it (ie deliver it) for their reply.

For further work in this popular area, we recommend using books dedicated to this genre, such as Paul Emmerson's *Email English* (Macmillan).

One issue is the disagreement on how accurate emails need to be. Should you spell-check an email? Native-speaker emails frequently contain mistakes, partly because they are often written at speed. In our view, emails should be fit for purpose, so an email to a friend need be far less accurate than an email to a prospective client, informing them of a new business service.

Using forums and bulletin boards

Asynchronous bulletin boards are useful, as participants have time to compose their messages, which may encourage attention to accuracy as well as 'deeper', more considered thinking than in synchronous exchanges. This chance to develop argumentation is a particularly important skill in EAP.

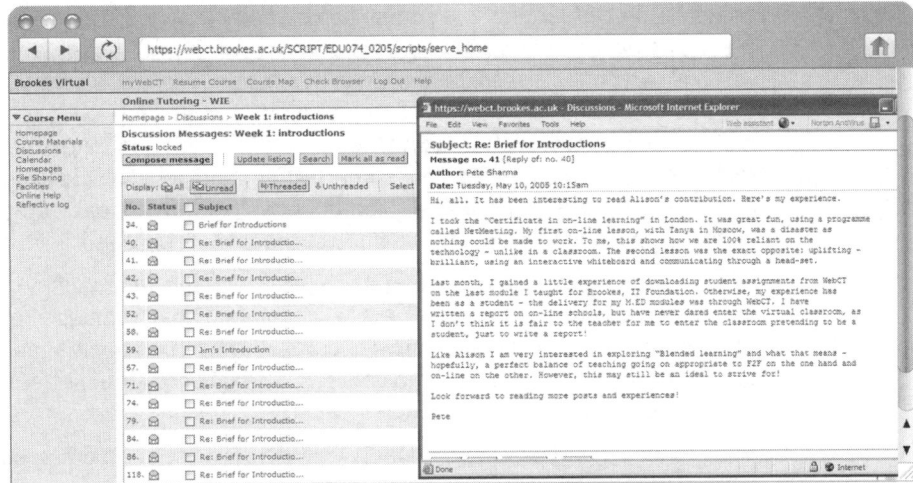

*Figure 8.9
Example of a
bulletin board
within a Virtual
Learning
Environment*

One opportunity offered by bulletin boards is the chance for your learners to communicate with a class in another country. Use a site such as: http://www.nicenet.org. This site offers the opportunity for learners to communicate with others through bulletin boards. Typical learner postings include questions such as 'What are the social problems in your country?'

Using video- and audio-conferencing

The main attraction of video-conferencing is that it saves people the time and expense of travel. It can bring together participants in a remote or isolated venue to experience a class. A freelance teacher has the opportunity of teaching an individual learner between their face-to-face classes. This may be a stand-alone course, or a supplement to a face-to-face course. Similar to video-conferencing and email, using Skype™ or other VoIP services offers learners a chance to communicate between classes.

Using Virtual Learning Environments (VLEs)

A VLE is a sophisticated learning platform. The benefits of using the individual asynchronous and synchronous tools have been looked at above. However, there are benefits to be gained when these different features are brought together in one system, and when you use CMC in conjunction with face-to-face teaching.

A VLE provides you with several advantages. It is a unifier of tools. There are almost innumerable possibilities to use blogs, wikis, forums, chats and even sites that will host material for you. However, a VLE brings this all under one roof, with tools that have been designed to work together and have the same design ethos, both pedagogically and visually. The effort in learning how to use these tools is therefore much reduced.

Using one platform makes the management of these tools much easier. You can administer blogs, wikis, etc much more easily, as they are all integrated into the management system of the VLE. Reports of how long individual learners have spent using the different elements of the course can be obtained, and support provided to those that are not using the VLE effectively. This support can include documents delivered by the VLE which would not be possible using individual tools. The VLE also enables you to contact the whole course, defined groups or individual learners very simply, and a community feeling can be developed by using these tools, the calendar and other functions. Building this community feeling, in which learners share and construct knowledge together, can be achieved in a number of ways. Learners can peer-review each others' assignments, for instance. One of the practical activities at the end of this chapter involves this activity.

Security is enhanced. There are real concerns with the vulnerability of young users of blogs and wikis that are usually freely accessible. Those running company courses will have to address sensitive security concerns of those companies, as there will inevitably be internal material being used in courses. A teacher or administrator has better control over these aspects with a VLE than if separate tools are used.

One of the biggest benefits of using a VLE is that it opens up the possibility of creating a blended-learning course involving face-to-face teaching, supported by online teaching using the synchronous and asynchronous tools within the system. A course can also be delivered purely online. Such a course, involving an e-moderator, is not the prime focus of this book.

Another benefit of a VLE is the opportunity it affords learners to access the course material at a time which suits them. In an EAP context, for example, learners can refer back to lecture notes which have been posted online, checking for any gaps in their own notes. The ability to do this seems to have a positive affect on performance. An EAP teacher can present a particular essay format in the lesson. Each learner in the class will be studying a different academic discipline. The teacher can post a range of sample essays on the VLE, each one from a different subject. This way, the learners only need read the content most appropriate to their course needs. The bank of essays on the VLE can be expanded and reused for each course.

Another possibility is the timed release of material. Some learners may be motivated to complete an online assignment if it is only available at a particular time. This feature allows you to drip-feed content. While there are benefits in reading ahead, allowing learners access to all the course material at the start of a course may prove overwhelming or distracting and even defeat the intermediate goals in the course.

Some learners are motivated by the type of instant feedback which can be provided by online assessments. Such feedback may help them build confidence, and feedback is not just limited to a score, but can explain wrong answers.

There are also benefits in the area of materials. Course materials can be reused and repurposed for the next course. Once you start designing and adapting materials for use in a VLE, you automatically make small adaptations to ensure reusability. Certain types of interactive exercises are relatively easy to produce quickly, such as a true/false quiz. The fact that such exercises are marked automatically may well save time.

Another opportunity afforded by a class VLE is that you can post the results of tasks undertaken by the learners, so they can be looked at by other members of the group. For example, when a group is studying presentation skills, you can post the digital videos of presentations, or presentations from previous learners. These examples of good practice may give learners models to work from, and an idea of what is required in terms of content.

Using a VLE has a great deal of potential. It provides you and your learners with both synchronous and asynchronous communication tools. The learning management system allows you to organize pre-existing content, and display new content. It incorporates tools for learner assessment. Finally, the password-protected environment contains administration functions which allow you to organize groups in terms of enrolling learners to courses, form groups and allocate teachers. The potential of a VLE is not only being explored by universities, but also by individual teachers, as in the final case study (see below).

Practical activities

A weekend with a friend from out-of-town

Acknowledgement for this idea: Sophie Ioannou-Georgiou

Aim: to develop general communicative competency, especially in expressing opinions.

Level: lower intermediate

Interaction: groups of four or five

Technology: chat room which you have made available on the Internet for your learners, eg Chatshack

Rationale: Learners have different levels of ability in the use of the four language skills. It may well be that those learners who are somewhat shy in speaking may express themselves more confidently and competently through the medium of writing. They may adopt an online persona, for instance. This activity encourages learners to interact without inhibitions in a small-group format through the medium of writing.

Before class: If your learners do not know how to use a chat room, you should schedule some time for them to get used to the basics of text chat. Print out handouts with the instructions of the task you are going to use in class (see page 147).

Procedure:

1 Explain the task to your learners: they are going to carry out a discussion entirely using text chat. They should discuss each idea offered by a member of the group and together decide what they should include in their final plan. Emphasize that they all have to agree on what they finally write down.

2 Elicit from the learners expressions they can use when they are discussing the task. Focus especially on expressions for stating opinions, such as *I believe, I agree with, I don't agree with* and *I think that,* and write these on the board.

3 Give the learners the handout and ask if there are any questions.

4 Have the learners log on to your chosen chat room.

5 The learners begin their chat. Monitor the activity, either through logging onto the chat room yourself or by wandering around the classroom.

6 Give learners a five-minute warning when time is nearly up so that they can round off their online discussions.

7 You may wish to give feedback on anything you noticed in terms of the use of language. It is also possible to print off the text of the discussion, read it later and give feedback in a future lesson.

Follow on: Either as homework or in class, the learners can write a diary entry on the day they spent with their friend and how their plan worked out.

Talky-writing

Aim: to raise awareness of the nature of writing emails

Level: intermediate and higher

Interaction: groupwork and feedback

Rationale: This activity first establishes some key differences between the skills of speaking and writing; it then naturally leads into raising awareness of the fact that emails combine features of both speaking and writing; emails have been described as 'talky-writing'. This activity is appropriate for Business English learners.

Technology: none necessary

Before class: Prepare and photocopy the worksheet (see page 148).

Procedure:

1 Hand out the worksheet and ask learners to list the key differences between speaking and writing.

2 Collate the learners' points on the board. Add any further distinctions (see the teachers' notes below).

3 Ask learners to complete the box on the worksheet, and list what they see as the characteristics of emails.

4 Elicit learner answers (see suggestions below). Ask learners any questions arising from the exercise, such as: Do they spell-check emails? What kind of emails do learners write, and how accurate do they have to be? Do they use abbreviations and emoticons? Are employees legally accountable for the content of their emails? etc.

Suggestions:	**Writing**	**Speaking**
	permanent	ephemeral
	one-way communication	two-way communication
	concise	includes repetition, hesitations
	complete sentences	includes incomplete sentences
	formal	informal
	no contractions	contractions

Emails

Use emoticons

Use abbreviations

Include formal and informal language

Contractions allowed

Pre-discussion task

Aim: to allow learners to prepare in advance of a discussion lesson; to practise the second form of the conditional

Level: intermediate and higher

Interaction: individual pre-lesson task; small-group work, whole-class work

Rationale: Some of the less confident learners will appreciate being able to think about a particular topic in advance of a fluency class, rather than being asked to give an opinion on the spur of the moment. Being able to prepare their thoughts may give them more confidence in class, and enable them to participate more.

Technology: VLE or email

Before class: Decide how far in advance of the lesson you wish to email participants and send a text such as the following. Include the name of a different crime (eg murder, kidnapping, robbery, mugging, etc) in each email.

We will be discussing crime and punishment in our next class. Consider the following crime (XXX) and decide on a suitable punishment (eg jail sentence, non-custodial sentence, a fine). Be ready to tell the group the punishment you have decided, and to find out whether they agree or not. Please check the meaning of any unknown words in this email before the class. Also, consider if the death penalty (capital punishment) is ever justified. You will find it helpful to study the language of agreeing and disagreeing in your coursebook.

Procedure:

1 Set up the discussion. Divide the class into small groups. Tell each group to choose a chairperson to moderate the discussion. Tell each learner to tell the group about their crime, and explain to them their preferred punishment and the reasons behind it. Each learner should find out what the other group members think about their sentence. The *If ...* form will naturally arise during the discussion. Encourage learners to reach an agreement on an appropriate sentence.

2 After the groups have finished their discussion, go systematically through the crimes and ask each group to give feedback on their punishment. Encourage whole-class discussion.

3 Give language feedback. If there is no time for this, post the feedback on the VLE.

Writing a business letter

Acknowledgement for this idea: Kevin Westbrook

Aim: to give learners practice in writing a business letter

Level: false beginner and higher

Interaction: face-to-face, online group work and feedback

Rationale: One of the potentials of using a VLE with your learners is to create a climate of collaboration and community. This can enable learners to learn from each other as much as from you; to allow learners to build knowledge through communicating with each other and challenging each other's ideas. This task allows peer feedback on a simple writing task and introduces learners to this collaborative form of learning.

Technology: VLE plus a range of other communication tools

Before class: Ensure that all learners can use the communication possibilities offered by the VLE and/or Skype™.

Procedure:

1 Provide some useful phrases used in a typical business letter. Give learners information on the layout of a typical letter. This can be done in class, and/or a model letter can be posted on the VLE.

2 Listening exercise: play the learners an audio extract of a telephone message involving a complaint.

3 Tell learners to write a letter in response to the telephone call.

4 Learners exchange letters with another learner for peer editing

5 Learners provide feedback on each others' letters using a convenient method for them (chat, Skype™, face-to-face, etc).

6 Learners revise their letters in the light of peer feedback. The revised letter can be submitted to you via the VLE for marking and comment.

7 You return the letter with comments, either in class or via the VLE.

Case studies

Case study 1:
Using chat in a language lesson

Sophie is a teacher in a secondary school. She decided to implement synchronous CMC with a monolingual class of 24 thirteen-year-old learners. The technological infrastructure at her school was not very good. She only had a low-bandwidth Internet connection, which limited her to using text chat with her learners. She explained to the learners how they would be using text chat in their classes and emphasized how the text-chat activities would be integral to the class. Netiquette and basic text-chat familiarization was achieved through relevant reading passages, which Sophie prepared and used in class as reading comprehension. Her reading texts also included screen shots of the chat programme she decided to use. This was a chat programme which she incorporated on her school's website.

She had five chat rooms so that her learners could work in small groups when online. Sophie wanted to keep her learners safe and undistracted while they were online during class, so she needed to have private chatrooms.

Sophie booked her school's only computer lab for one 45-minute period a week. The first session in the lab was dedicated to the learners' familiarization with the chat program. After that, the learners had a specific task to carry out each week. A learner from each group was in charge of saving the logs of the conversations, and sometimes the learners' homework involved taking the logs home and studying them for specific points which Sophie assigned.

The learners enjoyed these sessions very much and usually continued working away on the computers even after the bell had rung. Sophie says they needed to be 'dragged away' from the computers. She said she noticed her learners' motivation increasing and that this transferred to their regular class sessions. She was also very pleased with the shy learners' increased participation levels. Overall, Sophie believes that her learners' confidence in using English increased greatly due to these text-chat sessions.

Case study 2:
Supporting a course with Virtual Learning Environments

Sheila is a teacher and online course moderator, who works on a part-time basis for a university in Germany. She was teaching a group of learners, average age nineteen, who need to prepare their CVs for applying for jobs in an English-speaking country. Sheila first met her learners face to face in order to find out more about the kind of job applications they needed to make and how the process and the paperwork required was different from their own country (in this case, Germany). Among the areas she wished to cover on the course were CV writing, interview preparation and memo writing.

 Sheila made two decisions: firstly, to supplement the available published materials by devising her own, and secondly, to set up a VLE in order to provide the course with a degree of flexibility in terms of delivery. This meant she could take into account the learners' somewhat erratic work schedule. In her first trial, she used the freely available Internet Classroom Assistant Nicenet service. In her second attempt, she chose a more ambitious and complete solution: a Moodle platform. When she set up the VLE, Sheila was able to use email and have a class wiki space.

The course she devised consisted of four steps. In step 1, she provided her learners with their enrol key to log on to the VLE. She divided her learners into working groups. The learners accessed the job sites relevant to them, read two job adverts and decided which skills were needed. They collected the relevant information to help applicants such as themselves apply for a job in the UK or USA. They then imagined they were careers advisors and presented this information in the form of a list of tips under various headings: CV or résumé, covering letter and interview. The learners posted this information to the forums which Sheila had set up on the VLE.

In step 2, she asked the learners to work alone. They prepared their application and applied for one of the jobs by sending their application and covering letter by email to Sheila.

In step 3, the learners worked in small groups and prepared a list of interview questions.

In step 4, Sheila asked learners to imagine they were on the interviewing team. The learners looked at the applications forms. In the first trial, Sheila used applications from the original case study; in the second trial, she provided them with new candidate profiles that she felt were more appropriate to the jobs they were seeking themselves. The learners then chose the best candidate for the job. The final task involved writing a memo from the head of the interviewing team to the successful candidate. Sheila asked them to post their group's memo to the wiki space.

Sheila felt that there was great potential to expand and develop this project. She aims to use Skype™ calls to practise telephone interviews. Also, she would like her learners to record themselves and upload their audio files as podcasts. The next time she tries this project, she decided she will, in step 2, have learners send their interview questions to each other for checking first, rather than to her.

In this case study, Sheila's learners took on a variety of new roles and carried out tasks from a new perspective. This aspect of the case proved the most motivating, and encouraged the learners to make greater efforts. The feedback from learners suggested that they experienced satisfaction in completing a real-world and relevant task which achieved its purpose. They were effectively rehearsing a task for their own future. The blended formula involved a face-to-face induction session, four weeks' online work with e-tutor support, and a final face-to-face session. This flexibility was essential to the overall success of the project. Sheila felt that she was able to inform learners of each task by posting an announcement on the forum.

CREATING AND USING YOUR OWN RESOURCES

This chapter focuses on how to implement blended learning by creating your own resources in several ways. The methods in question are blogs, podcasts, wikis and websites, and each can be used, often for free or with minimum expense, to create materials for or to communicate with your learners. The degree of knowledge required varies, but all of these need you to invest time in both familiarizing yourself with the technology and then putting it to good use in and out of the classroom.

How to create your own resources

Blogs

Blog is short for *weblog*. A weblog is an online journal or diary. It consists of a chronological list of entries, or posts. These entries can contain text, photographs and links to other web pages. There are many millions of blogs on the Web, covering thousands of topics from the most intellectually challenging to the mundane.

Date of post

Title of post

Text of post

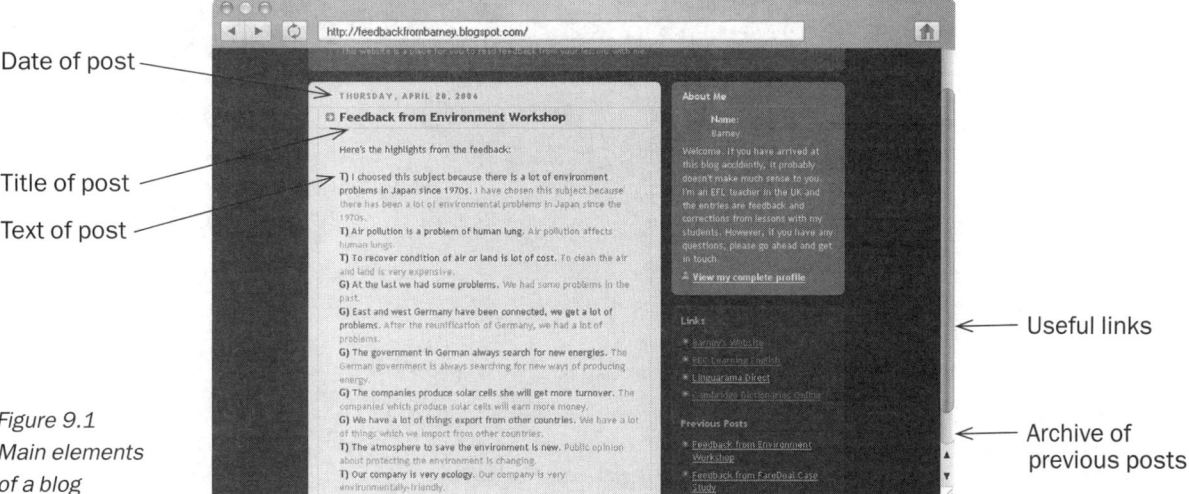

Useful links

Archive of previous posts

Figure 9.1
Main elements
of a blog

There are a growing number of blog services available on the Web. Some charge a fee, while others remain free or have different levels of service with different pricing. A good example is Blogger: http://www.blogger.com. Using Blogger, a blog can be set up and ready for use in seconds.

At the homepage of Blogger, click on 'Create your blog now'. To create an account, you need to choose a user name and a password. You will need these two pieces of information in order to access your blog whenever you wish to make a posting or make any other type of change. The display name you choose will be added to every blog posting you make. If you allow your learners to post entries to your blog, you can give each of them a different name which identifies who posted what.

The next stage is to give your blog a name. This will be displayed at the top of every page. You also need to choose a web address. With Blogger, each blog's URL is http://thename youchooseforyourblog.blogspot.com. This is the address which your learners will type into their browser to access the blog.

Whenever you make a change to your blog or post an entry, you will be asked to enter a series of random letters displayed on the screen. This is a security feature which prevents any software from hijacking your blog and making unwanted posts.

You are now ready to choose a template for the appearance of your blog. There are several ready-made templates and, in the short term, it is best to select one of these. If you do acquire some knowledge in HTML and web-page design at a later date, Blogger allows you to modify the templates or to create your own.

You are now ready to start blogging. Click on the Posting tab (see Figure 9.2). Every blog entry is made up of two basic parts: a title and the text. The name of the person who posted the entry and the time and date of the entry are added automatically when you post it. The text-entry window is like a simple word processor: you can choose from a small selection of fonts, and you can use bold and italics. You can also set the colour of the font use bullets, or create a numbered list. Hyperlinks can be created by clicking on the link button in the toolbar, which looks like a tiny globe with a chain link. To add pictures, click on the picture button, which is square and blue.

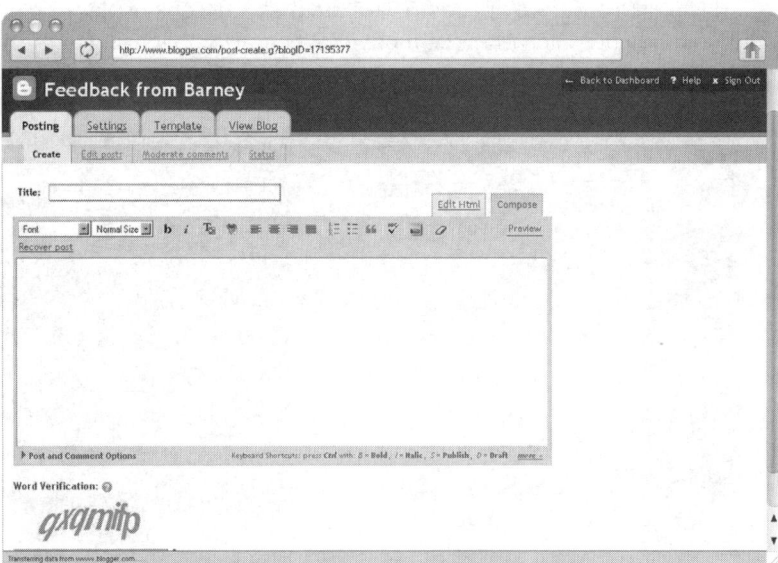

Figure 9.2
Posting an entry
on a blog

Once you have completed your blog entry, you can see how it will look on your blog by clicking on the Preview link at the top right of the text-entry box. If you want to make any changes, click on Compose to go back to the text-entry box. If you are happy that the post is ready to be added to the blog, enter the security code displayed at the bottom of the screen and click on Publish Post.

You can visit your blog by entering the URL you created or by clicking on the View Blog tab inside the Blogger website.

Readers of blogs, in this case your learners, can add comments to any entry. This is done by clicking on the Comment link at the bottom of the entry. This feature needs to be enabled, so check your blog settings before encouraging learners to comment. When you are logged onto Blogger to manage or post to your blog, click on the Settings tab then select Comments. Here you can control whether or not comments are displayed, who can add comments and, at the bottom of the page, set up an email notification so that, every time, someone adds a comment to a post on your blog, you receive an email with the text of the comment. This feature allows you to monitor any dialogue that may develop between your learners.

With Blogger, you can create team members. These are people who are allowed to contribute to the blog. You can make your learners team members, which allows them to post their own entries and to modify existing entries.

Other websites offering blog services include:

- WordPress (http://wordpress.com)
  Another free blogging service.
- six apart (http://www.sixapart.com)
- pMachine (http://www.pmachine.com)

These companies offer a number of online communication tools, including blogging software at a range of prices.

Podcasts

Podcasts are discussed in Chapters 2 and 3 in which we present some places on the Web where you can access podcasts to use with your learners or which your learners can use as self-study. Here, we look at creating your own podcasts to use with your learners.

There is a way of distributing podcasts over the Web using RSS which does not require you to have a website. The skills required to do this are beyond the scope of this book, but can be learned from *Podcasting Hacks: Tips and Tools for Blogging Out Loud* by Jack D. Herrington (O'Reilly, 2005).

Creating a podcast is not an activity for an elementary computer user. The following explanation is necessarily short and is intended to give an idea of how to proceed and, for those with the confidence and background, how to use these as the basis for their own experimentation. If you feel that it is not detailed enough for you but are determined to create podcasts for your learners, then we advise you to buy a book such as the one recommended above and make use of the detailed guide it offers.

There are two fundamental items of equipment you require: a sound card and a microphone. If your computer has speakers, then it has a sound card and will also have a socket to allow you to connect a microphone. Use the best one available that you can afford. If you are going to be the only voice on the podcast, you can use a clip-on microphone like those you see used on TV programmes. If you plan to have several people speaking together, you will need an omni-directional microphone which picks up sound from all around it.

To record a podcast and then convert it into an mp3 file for distribution, you require two pieces of software: the recorder and the mp3 encoder. The two proposed here are free and can be used at both a basic and advanced level. The installation files of the programs can be downloaded from the following websites:

- Audacity (http://audacity.sourceforge.net)
  Audacity is used to record and edit digital audio.
- LameFE (http://lamefe.nauta-clarus.de/index.php?download)
  This is an mp3 encoder that integrates well with Audacity. It is used to convert the recordings you create with Audacity into mp3 files that can be played by computer media players, digital music players and some types of PDAs and mobile phones (see Chapter 7).

Once you have decided to record a podcast, it is advisable to spend as much time as possible preparing a script or, if you feel you have the skill to extemporise well, detailed notes to help you on your way. It is worth having a dry run before making the final recording, especially if you intend to use more than one voice in your podcast.

1 Once you have prepared and rehearsed your content and are ready to record, connect your microphone to your computer and open Audacity.

2 To start recording, click on the red record button at the top of the program window. As you speak, the program will automatically adjust the input level to avoid distortion. The recording is represented as a sound-wave graphic that grows as you speak.

3 When you reach the end of your script, click on the stop button. You can now click on the play button to review your recording.

4 If there any sections which you wish to remove, you can highlight that section of the sound wave and press Delete on your keyboard. If you wish to add anything or rerecord something you have deleted, open a new file and record the extra material, highlight it and copy it. Then return to the main recording, click in the sound wave at the point at which you wish to add the new material and click on Paste.

5 When you are happy with your recording, first save it as an Audacity file.

6 Now you can convert the recording to the mp3 audio format. Click on the File menu and select Export as MP3. After you click on Save, you can add ID information. This is the information that you see displayed when you play an audio file on your computer's media player or your portable mp3 player.

7 The mp3 file is now ready to distribute to your learners. The size of the mp3 file depends on the length of the recording. Using the default settings of the software, one minute of audio is roughly 1Mb, ie a twenty-minute podcast will be 20Mb.

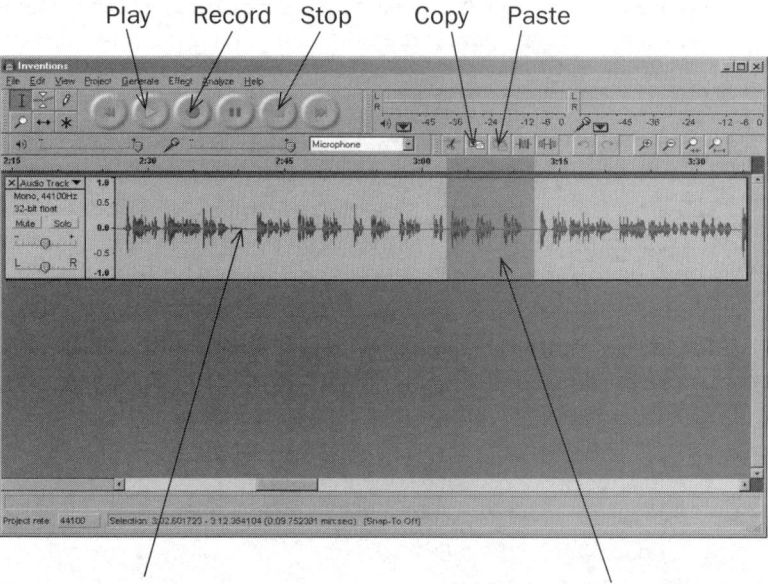

Figure 9.3
The main features of the Audacity audio recording and editing program

Soundwave of the recording   Highlighted section to be deleted or copied

Wikis

A wiki is a website on which the pages can be edited by the users, as well as the creator of the website. The users can change the content by adding or removing information, or editing the existing content. The best-known wiki is Wikipedia (see http://www.wikipedia.org), a web-based encyclopaedia. This has grown exponentially due to the collaborative efforts of enthusiasts around the world to become a leading repository of knowledge. The collaborative nature of Wikipedia, with users across the globe providing content, sharing knowledge and commenting on other users' input, provides an insight into the nature of wikis. Wikis offer learners the chance to collaborate on tasks outside the language classroom.

Setting up a wiki can be as straightforward as setting up a blog. If you would like to set up a wiki, there are a number of easy ways of doing this. Try one of the following sites:
- PB wiki (*PB* stands for *peanut butter*) (http://pbwiki.com)
- Edit this (http://www.editthis.info)
- Wiki spaces (http://www.wikispaces.com)

During the process of setting up your wiki, you will be asked to make some decisions, such as supplying the website address you would like your wiki site to have. Another choice is whether you would like to make your site available to anyone on the Web, or if you prefer to restrict access and editing to only those who know the password. The second may be your preferred option if you are setting up a class wiki. There may be a hosting charge for having a private wiki.

Using a wiki and making changes to the content is largely intuitive. Whenever you add content, you will need to create a page and save it. After the page has been created, anyone can edit it, usually by clicking on Edit page. When you have finished making changes, simply click on Save changes. One of the ways of editing a page is to click on a word and then create a hyperlink to a new page. It is possible to see the history of changes made to the page. To do this, click on the History button.

Many wiki owners are content with a simple wiki. There are also a number of ways you can make your wiki more attractive, such as adding pictures or a logo.

A useful wiki which is designed to discuss writing on wikis can be found at http://www.seedwiki.com/wiki/wikiwritingworkshop.

Websites

Creating a good-looking, easy-to-use website from scratch continues to be an undertaking that requires some specialist knowledge, especially if you wish to do more than simply display information. However, if you have a general sympathy for and openness to computer-based systems, there are many books and websites that can help you acquire the basics. There are also software packages that can help you build a website. Be warned, however, that even with this type of software, an understanding of the HTML code that is used to create web pages is necessary.

Opportunities and issues

Using blogs

These offer many opportunities to language teachers because they are easy to set up and operate and can be an effective way of communicating with learners outside lesson time. They also allow the learner the opportunity to do extra work, so the use of technology can consolidate and extend the classroom work, an ideal blended-learning approach. Here, we will focus on a number of ways of integrating blogs into the courses you teach. This list is not exhaustive, and you will probably have your own ideas for using blogs. You can also use the blog project planning sheet on page 149.

Pre-teaching

If classroom time is limited, you can use a blog to make vocabulary available to learners before the lesson. Make sure you have agreed this procedure with them before you do this and that you have time to honour the agreement yourself.

A blog can have a mailing list. This means that when you post a new entry, it is emailed to everyone on the list. If you agree to use the blog to pre-teach, this can be a very useful feature. However, learners will need to agree to provide their email addresses, and you must remember to update the mailing list if and when learners leave or join the group, or the group finishes.

Developing language

Traditional vocabulary lists are very static. Whether you are providing vocabulary as feedback or before lessons or simply as useful input, the use of hyperlinks can inject an element of interactivity.

Hyperlinks can be attached to individual words or groups of words, such as fixed functional expressions or idioms. These hyperlinks can take learners directly to that word's entry in an online dictionary or to the definition of an idiom on websites dedicated to that type of language. Expressions can be linked to searches using tools such as Google or Yahoo. Words can even be linked to web pages that contain photographs or images that might help to illustrate and elucidate the vocabulary item in question. The same can be done with functional language and expressions.

Pictures and diagrams are very useful in language teaching and can be incorporated into blog entries. One technique is to photograph the whiteboard at the end of brainstorming sessions with your learners. You can then transfer the image from your digital camera straight to a blog post. Choose the largest image size Blogger allows so that the writing in the photograph is legible.

If you have some experience with using graphic-design software, you can create diagrams such as time-lines to illustrate grammar points (see Figure 9.3). Many learners find these very helpful, so you can include them as part of blog posts when posting feedback on grammar mistakes.

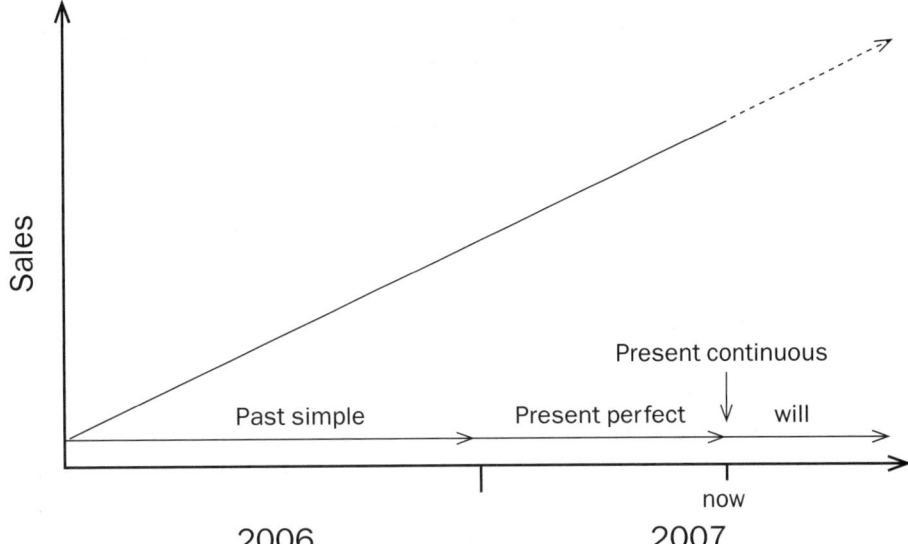

Figure 9.3
Time-line diagram
created using
graphic-design
software to be
added to a blog
post

There are a couple of ways of handling pronunciation using a blog. One is to cut and paste the phonemic spelling of the word from a CD-ROM dictionary. Unfortunately, while this can work quite well, some browsers do not display the phonemic characters correctly. The other method is to make a hyperlink to an online dictionary that has a pronunciation feature, allowing learners to hear a model.

Giving feedback

Some fluency lessons can generate large quantities of written feedback. Often there is not enough time to go through all this feedback in the classroom; alternatively, you, as the teacher, would like time to filter the feedback, or you want to share this feedback with your learners but do not want the process to eat into the time of the next lesson. Using a blog takes the pressure off you to finish the lesson with a detailed and legible feedback sheet, but also makes sure that the feedback is available to your learners before the start of the next lesson.

If you use a blog for feedback, you need your learners' agreement to post their mistakes on the Web. It is advisable to not use names on the blog, but to identify learners by initials if it is necessary to do so. Although a blog is accessible to anyone with an Internet connection, it is extremely unlikely that anyone will find your feedback blog by accident. You can demonstrate this to yourself and your learners by using a search engine to search for it from the point of view of someone who does not know the specific content of the blog.

Promoting learner autonomy

Using a blog can establish good practices of learner autonomy. Learners have to be proactive in accessing the information you have posted to the blog and following the links to online resources. It also important to state this directly when you introduce the blog as part of the course. You may also need to support your learners by helping them to develop their web-searching skills. See Chapter 2 for more information on effective searching techniques.

Communicating between lessons

Using the comments feature, learners can provide feedback on the blog entry. They can add their own ideas, thoughts, vocabulary, etc. A dialogue can start between individual learners, or between learners and yourself. If you wish to promote this type of communication, a good fluency lesson is a discussion on what is acceptable and unacceptable use of this feature. As owner of the blog, you have control over the comments feature and can delete any comments you feel are inappropriate or unhelpful.

With blog services, you can create team members. These are people who are allowed to contribute to the blog. You can make your learners team members, which allows them to post their own entries and to modify existing entries. This is a possibility for a long-term group, but needs to have very strict rules that the members agree to abide by. The discussion to establish the rules and the committing of those rules to paper (or the blog) is a very effective group activity.

Exercises

If you use a blog as a way of communicating with learners between lessons, then you can create personalized exercises that they can complete as self-study or homework. The main benefit is that entries with exercises can be posted at any time between the end of one lesson and the start of the next. Compared to some of the online exercises discussed in Chapter 3, exercises on a blog provide limited interactivity. This can take the form of hyperlinks to dictionaries or sources of information or, occasionally, the answer.

The best kind of exercises to place on a blog involve texts. These can be used to create a gap-fill exercise, or you can remove elements of the text such as articles or auxiliary words. Vocabulary can be substituted or mixed up. For lower levels, paragraphs can be mixed up, or learners asked to match headings to paragraphs. Make sure you give the learners clear instructions to print the exercise and about what they need to do to complete it.

Since a blog is a web-based resource, if your learners or institution have computers equipped with a CD-ROM dictionary, the QuickFind feature can be used in conjunction with reading the blog or doing any exercises that have been incorporated into entries (see Chapter 4).

Exercises can be reused with subsequent groups of learners. Every blog post has a web address, and you can add a hyperlink to an entry within your own blog that contains an exercise you created at an earlier date.

Using podcasts

Good podcasts require two basic elements: good sound quality and interesting, useful content. The first depends on the equipment and software you use, the latter on having a clear idea about the purpose and audience for the podcast and good preparation.

As a language teacher, there are a number of excellent reasons why you would want to record podcasts for your learners. The first of these is to provide listening practice that is specifically tailored to the needs of your learners or to fit with the course your are delivering. You can record monologues or, with the help of a colleague, dialogues that provide context-based models of grammar or vocabulary that is to be used in forthcoming lessons or recycled from a previous lesson. Podcasts created by teachers can often simply be models of native-speaker pronunciation and accent for learners who do not have the opportunity for regular exposure.

A podcast can focus more specifically on pronunciation and can be written and recorded to meet the exact needs of a learner or group of learners. The models of the sounds and words that the learner needs to practise can be based on examples and placed into a context given in a class. This type of podcast does not need to be more than a few minutes long. As well as the models, it can have reminders of any advice given by the teacher in class. The convenience of the mp3 format and the tailored nature of this type of podcast produces effective results amongst learners determined to address their pronunciation issues.

As suggested above, a podcast can be used to pre-teach and give input in a format other than a written one. Learners who are more aural than visual in their learning style appreciate and benefit from explanations of grammar and vocabulary which are delivered verbally. This could also be a way of delivering information to learners who have missed a lesson.

A more advanced use of podcasts involves combining a recording of a fluency activity, such as a class discussion or role-play, with recorded comments and language feedback. This will involve some audio-editing skills. Although this is not technically difficult using a program like Audacity, it can be very time-consuming.

If you decide to create podcasts for your learners to use, they do not have to be distributed over the Web. You can email shorter podcasts to learners or store longer ones on your school's computer network where they can accessed from any computer within the school. If your learners have mp3 players, you can transfer the podcast directly to those.

Using wikis

One of the most powerful benefits of using wikis in language learning is as a collaborative tool. Potentially, everyone in a group could work at changing and editing a document and work towards a final version of a particular text. This can help develop bonds between members of the class and create a community spirit. The premise here is that the learners can learn from each other, and learn through their interactions with other group members.

One of the interesting features of wikis is that they blur the distinction between author and audience. Rather than somebody owning a document, its composition becomes a joint effort. A text can be rewritten many times, and anyone in the class can make changes. For a teacher interested in studying the process of writing, a wiki may provide valuable insights into how learners arrive at a final version of a text. This can be done by tracking the changes made to a particular page.

A wiki could allow your class to share notes. The whole group can brainstorm a topic area online in advance of a class. The wiki could be a place where learners communicate with each other outside lessons, replicating some of the benefits of a VLE (see Chapter 8).

There are a number of exciting activities which can be done using wikis. One idea called 'branching story' taps into the imagination of learners. The story in question could be a fantasy story (rescue the maiden, kill the dragon or run away) or involve a moral dilemma. You start the story with an introduction, then leave the protagonist of the story with three choices. By clicking on one of the options, the learner is taken to a new page in the wiki. The learner then becomes the writer, and he or she continues the story. Once again, three choices are offered at the end of the next part. The final result will be a moral maze created by the group. This activity has proved especially popular with young adults, as it taps into creativity and practises writing with a purpose.

A real-world outcome to a task could motivate some learners. You could brainstorm areas of interest – such as a rock band, a town you love, or a famous person – or an area of expertise, and then collate a list on the whiteboard. The learners then go to Wikipedia to check the entry. Is it accurate? Is it complete? They then report back on their findings. As a follow-up, some learners may wish to contribute to the encyclopedia. Note that some restrictions now apply to changing certain entries on Wikipedia.

One key issue is that activities using wikis involve ceding a degree of control to the learners. If everyone can change a web page, there is potential for an element of disagreement; in a worst-case scenario, learners may be unhappy at the changes implemented by a colleague. To avoid this, it is wise to be judicious in setting wiki tasks. You may wish to appoint a group leader, whose editorial decision is final. It is worth considering that not all learners like their work changed by peers. The concept of collaborative learning may also be one that is difficult to grasp by some learners. Fortunately, instances of malicious use of wikis seem to be rare.

Building websites

The most pertinent question here is whether or not having a website is something that could be useful for you as a language teacher. The answer may prompt you to go down the road of building, or paying someone else to build, a website. From the point of view of a freelance teacher, this may make commercial sense, as a website can be an effective way of marketing your services. Although you can register a unique domain name, which is the first part of a web address, there is an annual fee to maintain the ownership of this, and you will also have to pay a fee to a hosting company that will place your website on a server that is accessible to web users. Teachers working for large educational institutions, such as a university, are often able to place a personal website within the website of that institution. If you are looking to use the Web to communicate with your learners outside of the classroom, the simplest solution is setting up a blog which is extremely straightforward, less time consuming and cheaper.

Practical activities

Blogs

Giving feedback

Aim: to provide language feedback on classroom fluency activities when there is insufficient time during lessons

Level: elementary to advanced

Interaction: whole class then individual

Technology: blog

Rationale: After a fluency activity, you do not always have time to give detailed feedback. A blog can be used to provide learners with written feedback. Since a blog is on the Web, you can add the feedback, and learners can access it at any time from any computer linked to the Internet.

Procedure:

1 Introduce the idea of placing feedback on a blog. Explain the benefits of having this information accessible between lessons rather than wait until the next lesson.

2 Decide how to organize the feedback. The best way is to present issues based on the following and ask the learners whether they have any other suggestions.

- What colours to use: for example, black for the mistakes, with proposed corrections in red; grammar mistakes in blue, vocabulary mistakes in green, and so on.
- Whether or not the feedback should identify who said what by the use of initials.
- How much feedback should be posted. As much as possible or only the most important points?
- How soon the feedback should be posted after a lesson. This depends on you and your schedule.

3 Once the organization has been decided, agree on a trial period during which you and the class will use this system.

4 At the end of this period, you and the class review the success or otherwise of the feedback blog and discuss any necessary changes or whether to discontinue its use.

Follow on: If the blog is a success, its uses can be expanded to some of those outlined below.

Teaching vocabulary

Aim: to provide support for learning vocabulary

Level: elementary to advanced

Interaction: whole class then individual

Technology: blog

Rationale: A blog can be used to pre-teach vocabulary, to give feedback on mistakes, and to demonstrate using an online dictionary as a vocabulary-learning tool. This activity presupposes that the learners involved are already familiar with using a blog as part of their language learning. See the *Giving feedback* activity above for details on how to introduce a blog to your learners.

Procedure:

1 Take a mistake frequently made by your learners, for example, confusing the words *summarize* and *resume*.

2 Create a blog posting which presents these two words in context, such as a sentence or short piece of text.

3 Use another web browser window to go to an online dictionary such as http://dictionary.cambridge.org and look up *resume*. Once you have the definition displayed, highlight and copy the address of that web page from the address box at the top of the browser window.

4 Return to the unfinished blog entry; highlight the word *resume* within the text and click on the Link button; paste the address of the dictionary page into the link box and click OK. This creates a hyperlink from the word *resume* in your blog posting to the definition in the online dictionary.

5 You can now repeat the procedure for the word *summarize*.

6 Make sure the rubric of the entry instructs your learners to click on the links and note the difference between the two words.

7 Once you have added the hyperlinks, you can post the entry to your blog.

Follow on: Make sure you refer to the blog posting in a subsequent class in case there are any questions from your learners. You should also do a fluency activity during which your learners have the opportunity to demonstrate whether they can use the words correctly.

A further development of this is to link to online pronunciation models. For American English, you can link to the Answers.com online dictionary. For example, the link http://opera.answers.com/police goes to a dictionary entry for the word *police* which includes an audio clip of the pronunciation.

Teaching idioms

Aim: to provide support for learning idioms

Level: advanced

Interaction: whole class then individual

Technology: blog

Rationale: This is another activity which uses hyperlinks from a blog entry to a resource on the Web. This activity presupposes that the learners involved are already familiar with using a blog as part of their language learning. See the *Giving feedback* activity above for details on how to introduce a class to using a blog.

Procedure:

1 Take an idiom or set of idioms that you want your learners to learn or be familiar with.

2 Create a blog entry which lists these idioms but without any explanation.

3 Highlight each idiom in turn and create a hyperlink to the definition of that idiom in *Using English.com Dictionary of Idioms and Idiomatic Expressions:* http://www.usingenglish.com/reference/idioms.

4 In a subsequent lesson, test your learners on the meanings of the idioms or challenge them to use the idioms appropriately in a fluency activity such as a role-play.

Variation: A more demanding modification of stage 3 is to create a hyperlink from the idiom in the blog entry to a search engine. Go to Google and place the idiom inside double quotation marks, for example "know the ropes". Then copy the web address of the Google search results page and use this as the link for the expression in the blog entry (see Figure 9.4). When your learners click on this type of link, they have to choose a website from the search results which explains the idiom and then find a good example of the idiom in use to present in class.

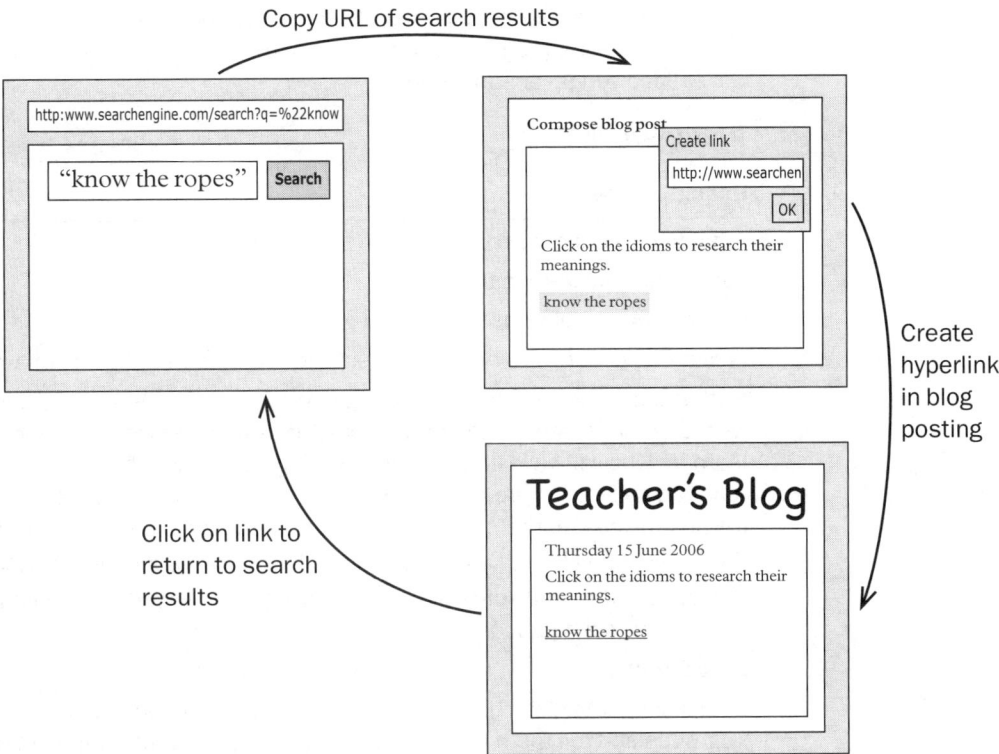

Figure 9.4
Creating a link
in a blog to search-
engine results

Exercises for homework

Aim: to provide homework activities

Level: elementary to intermediate

Interaction: whole class then individual

Technology: blog

Rationale: This activity is way of providing extra exercises to your learners between classes. You need to agree with your learners about when and how often these types of exercises are posted to the blog and the mechanism for following them up, either via the blog or in class time. This example uses texts. They can either be copied and pasted from another website or created by you with the answer posted in a subsequent blog entry.

Procedure:

1 Copy the text you have selected into a blog entry then create a gap-fill by removing words and replacing them with underscore symbols.

2 Add a list of the words you have removed below the text. For a more challenging exercise, you can exclude this part. However, this only works if your learners have read the text earlier or are very familiar with the vocabulary of the subject matter.

3 If you have copied the text from another website, provide a hyperlink to the source of the text. If you have created the text yourself, wait until the period you have agreed with your learners elapses, and then add the complete text to a new blog entry.

4 The rubric for the exercise should be included in the blog entry. Learners should be instructed to print the entry and attempt the exercise on paper. Once they have completed it to their satisfaction, they can click on the link to the original text and compare it with their version.

Variations: Alternative exercises with texts include ordering sentences, matching headings to paragraphs, or quizzes. You need to make it clear to your learners how these will be followed up or assessed.

Podcasts

Podcast project

Aim: to create podcasts

Level: intermediate to advanced

Interaction: whole class and small groups

Technology: software and equipment required for creating a podcast

Rationale: This is project-style activity which can be scheduled to take place over several weeks or the length of the entire course. It works best with technologically literate learners who will have little trouble learning how to use the software and equipment required and can, therefore, focus their efforts on the language content of the project. It also provides learners with a degree of autonomy to create something of interest to themselves and their peer group. See the Podcast project planning sheet on page 150.

Before class: Spend some time familiarizing yourself with the equipment and software required to make podcasts.

Procedure:

1 Explain to the class that they are going to create podcasts. Divide the class into small groups and tell them to discuss and agree on the topic of their podcast.

2 Issue the Project Planning Sheet (see page 150) to each group and ask them to fill out as many of the parts as they can at this stage. How the podcast is to be delivered can be considered later in the project. Introduce the class to a program such as Audacity and show how it can be used to record and edit audio.

3 The groups prepare scripts for their podcasts. This can be done in class or as homework. You can provide as much language support as they need at this stage.

4 The groups record their podcasts. If they have access to the necessary equipment (computer with sound card and microphone) at home, it can be done as homework. Otherwise school equipment can be used.

5 The recordings are edited and any music and sound effects added. The finished podcasts are converted into mp3 format. At this stage, a decision needs to be made about delivery. This can be done using a school network, CD-ROMs or mp3 players.

6 Each group listens to the podcasts of the other groups, and then gives its evaluation of the other podcasts. This can be done as a class discussion or using the Podcast evaluation sheet (see page 139).

Variations: The class can create a single magazine-style podcast with short reports from each group which are joined together to make a single programme. This type of podcast will still need a presenter to introduce it and do the links between the reports. You could hold a class election to chose the person to do this.

Wikis

Questioning a text

Acknowledgement for this idea: Tilly Harrison

Aim: to raise awareness of the possibilities of using a wiki in class

Level: intermediate and higher

Interaction: whole class and homework

Technology: wiki

Rationale: This task is designed to show the collaborative possibilities of using a wiki. It allows learners time to process and question a text in advance of a lesson. This reveals areas that the learners may need to work on, providing a focus for the face-to-face class. By selecting a particularly dense or challenging text, the learners will benefit from each others' contributions, fostering an idea of working together to understand the text. In other words, they can learn from each other.

Before class: Set up a wiki using Wikispaces. Have the URL available to distribute to your learners. Post a text on the website for learners to read and edit. In an EAP context, this could be an introductory text about the course.

Procedure:

1 In the face-to-face class, provide the address of the wiki and tell your learners to visit it and read the first text. If there is something they do not understand in the text, they can add a comment. You will need to check that learners know how to do this, either through an in-class demonstration, or by creating a handout with the relevant instructions. Ask the class to visit the site two or three times during the week, and to try and add a comment or explanation to any queries they find from others in the class.

2 Before the next lesson, visit the site and see which areas learners have had problems with. Click on History to view the site changes.

3 In the follow-up class, deal with the areas which remain unsolved. Tell learners that the time you spend in class dealing with the text may well be reduced because of the pre-work they have done. This will inform the learners of the benefits of working on a text outside the lesson, and encourage them to use the wiki during the course in a similar way.

Variations: Post a list of learner mistakes on the wiki. Ask learners to correct at least one before the next lesson. Deal with any errors which your learners have not been able to answer.

Case studies

Case study 1:
Using blogs as a student diary

James teaches at a language school where he had a small group of adult learners who were to meet and learn together for a year. He proposed that the group set up an ongoing project that they could take responsibility for and could be used to track their progress.

After some discussion, the group agreed to set up a blog which they would use as a joint learning diary. Each person in the group was a team member and could post to the blog and modify existing posts. The group discussed the etiquette of the blog and wrote a set of rules by which they all agreed to abide. This became the first entry on the blog.

The group established a rota and took it in turns to post a summary of each lesson they had together. The other members could add comments to this summary or challenge its accuracy. At the beginning of each lesson, the comments were reviewed and changes made to the post. James' responsibility was to monitor the content of the blog posts and any comments and provide language feedback when the group met.

As the course progressed, it became apparent that some members of the group were more dedicated to the blog than others. The main issues with the rota were people who failed to make the entry when it was their turn or posted their entry very late and so it was displayed out of sequence. Other members of the group used the comment feature to say things that were unhelpful and occasionally not in English. After a couple of months, James proposed a discussion to consider the blog and whether the group should continue to use it. Those in favour of continuing used entries from the blog itself to demonstrate how it could be used to track their improvement. Eventually, it was agreed that those who found the blog useful could continue to write entries, and James would continue to monitor and provide feedback. However, the content of the blog would only be discussed once a month, instead of every lesson.

The blog persisted throughout the entire course. As the archive built up, James was able to refer to specific entries as a way of reviewing what had been covered during the course. As the year came to a close, the main proponents of the blog within the group gave a presentation in which they showed sample entries from the blog throughout the year to demonstrate the progress they had made.

Case study 2:
Creating podcasts to support pronunciation work

Laura teaches a single-language class of learners who all have similar pronunciation issues. An informal group discussion revealed that every member of the class had some sort of electronic device on which they could play mp3 audio files. She proposed to provide them with a specially created listening task in the form of a podcast which she could distribute electronically and they could listen to on whatever device was most convenient for each of them. The group readily agreed to this. It was decided that the easiest way to distribute the podcast was for Laura to email it to each learner. She took everyone's email address and commited to sending the first podcast before the next lesson. The learners promised to listen to it and be ready with their comments

Laura carefully scripted a short monologue with lots of examples of the sounds that presented difficulties to her learners. This script included a brief introduction reminding the listener of the purpose of the recording. Using the Audacity software and a clip-on microphone, she recorded this script. The recording consisted of the script, followed by models of individual words that had presented problems for her learners and were part of the script, and then the script again. She found she had to experiment with the position of the microphone before she could get a recording that she thought was clear enough for her learners to hear the differences between some of the minimal pairs modelled in the podcast.

When she had finished, the entire recording was about seven minutes. She used LameFE to convert the Audacity file into the mp3 format. The resulting file was about 6.5Mb and was small enough to be emailed to each of her learners.

The next time the group met, she got their feedback on the usefulness of the podcast. On the whole, the comments were very positive. In fact, most of the class were extremely enthusiastic. The only negative comments came from the one learner who Laura knew had the most difficulty with the pronunciation and who said he was unable to hear the difference between the sounds on the recording. The lesson then continued with a pronunciation exercise to directly practise the target sounds, during which she gave extra support to the learner who had difficulty understanding the podcast. This was followed by short role-plays using words from the podcast.

Laura asked the class whether they thought it was worthwhile her recording more podcasts. They all said it was a good idea. Laura suggested that she did one or two a month and reminded them that they could retain each one on their mp3 players and listen as often they wished or felt they needed to.

Limiting the number saved Laura from a lot of extra work but also meant that each podcast was an event and, therefore, got the full attention of her learners when it was emailed to them. As the course continued, their pronunciation steadily improved. Although she could not say for sure whether this was as a result of the podcasts, Laura was certain that they had helped to raise her learners' awareness of their pronunciation mistakes.

Case study 3:
Using a wiki to create a virtual vocabulary notebook

Acknowledgement for this case study: Tilly Harrison

Sally is an EAP teacher, working at a British university. She set up a wiki in order to expand the vocabulary of her learners. The learners needed to read challenging texts, but were often daunted by the amount of new vocabulary necessary to understand these texts. Each learner was asked to add one new word a week to the class wiki. They added a context sentence from their reading, the source of the text, a definition and a personal comment, or further sentence containing the word. By clicking on the link, the class members could visit the definition page. Each week during the course, she asked a few learners to present their words to the class. This way, she felt better able to comment on the appropriacy of the examples.

Sally is generally pleased with the way the project has gone. The words chosen by the learners were, on the whole, relevant to the group and the course. At first, she offered to help create the pages, but realized that with a class of 30, she was doing too much work. Next year, she will take the class into the self-access centre and have the technically minded learners help the weaker ones. Looking at the learner feedback forms on her pilot project, Sally felt that not all learners were good at choosing words, or appreciated the reliance on their classmates for input, which they preferred to come from her. Overall, she felt the wiki project was a success and that the class benefited from the existence of a virtual notebook. While they only contributed one word a week, they felt that the virtual notebook contained a lot of useful and relevant lexis, and gave them a good return on the time invested.

AFTERWORD: A BRIEF LOOK AT THE FUTURE

This book has looked at using technology inside and outside the classroom. It has described blended-learning courses which combine a face-to-face teaching component with appropriate support using technology. It assumes that you play a role in the teaching and learning of a language, and that the technology can enhance and complement that role. This paradigm, in our view, is a model which can be applied equally well to technologies in the future.

We have seen that technology has changed forever what we do as language teachers; it has opened up new opportunities for the way our learners learn. Nowadays, our teaching role is far wider than inputting new knowledge. We also facilitate learning. While our learners study or communicate using technology, we monitor activities and ensure that learning opportunities are maximized. We run learner-training sessions, informing learners of the potential of technology, and encourage our learners to take advantage of the many opportunities to practise away from the confines of the classroom.

What about the future? We may speculate on some trends with a degree of relative certainty; other trends are far more uncertain, and even impossible to guess. We can state fairly confidently that the future holds more of the same. The trend of 'ubiquity' refers to the fact that the number of computers, hand-held devices and technologies in general will continue to grow. Schools will buy more electronic projectors; online materials will proliferate; teachers will support their learners' efforts with blogs, wikis and VLEs such as Moodle. Electronic dictionaries will take advantage of the greater storage space provided by DVD. We can expect technologies to become smaller, faster and cheaper.

Technology changes and develops quickly. It has been said that it is dangerous to make predictions more than two years ahead. In two years' time, some teachers and learners will be using technologies which don't exist today. Our children will be using technologies which we cannot even imagine. History is littered with examples of wildly inaccurate prophecies. If we try and predict too far into the future, we quickly end up in the realm of science fiction. Just how far technology will develop in areas such as AI (artificial intelligence), machine translation, virtual reality, gaming and speech recognition is unclear. How far such developments will impact on the teaching and learning of languages is equally unclear. We only know that change is inevitable, and in our view, welcome.

Stephen Bax has written about the 'normalization' of technology. This is a time when a technology is used in a wholly appropriate way, and is so taken for granted that it becomes 'invisible'. So, let us conclude with a example of 'normalization'. One of our colleagues is fairly technophobic and somewhat resistant to the change technology inevitably brings to teaching. He teaches EAP. He was looking at the needs-analysis sheets for his new group. He automatically turned to the Internet, and began typing in the specialist subjects his learners needed to study into Google, in order to research for material. This strikes us as a wholly appropriate use of technology. It goes beyond whether you feel positive or negative towards technology. It is simply led by the learners, and is wholly practical. Moreover, it is taken for granted that the typical staffroom has computers available for teachers. Increasing numbers of institutions have computers – indeed, learning technologies – available for learners.

Technology will continue to play a part in our lives as teachers. The future will be exciting. If the new technologies lead to better learning outcomes, then that is a good thing for teachers and learners.

APPENDIX 1 | TEACHER'S RESOURCE BANK

Resource	Chapter	Page
Authentic text gap-fill	2	134
Webquest template	2	135
London visit webquest	2	136
American accents	2	137
Collocation finder	2	138
Podcast evaluation worksheet	2, 9	139
Podcast lesson preparation sheet	2	140
Evaluation sheet for use with web-based material	3	141
Exploring word frequency	4	142
Using dictionaries	4	143
Mapping words	4	144
Portable electronic dictionaries	4	145
Email template	8	146
A weekend with a friend from out-of-town	8	147
Talky-writing	8	148
Blog project planning sheet	9	149
Podcast project planning sheet	9	150

Authentic text gap-fill (Chapter 2)

You are going to find a text on the Web and use it to create a gap-fill exercise for other members of your group.

1 You need to agree a topic with the other members of your group.

   Topic:_____

2 Now use a search engine to find an article about this topic that you think is interesting. Make sure that the article is not too long or too short. It should not be more than one page long when you print it.

3 Copy the text from the web page and paste it into a word-processor document.

4 Decide what words you are going to remove from the text. You could remove new words, or prepositions or adjectives, or you could remove every seventh or tenth word.

5 When you have selected the words, use *cut* to remove them and *paste* to put them at the bottom of the page. Do not forget to put an empty space like this – _____ – in the places where you removed the words.

6 When you have completed your gap-fill, make a print out and bring it plus a copy of the original article back to the group.

Webquest template (Chapter 2)

Introduction

Task

Process

Resources

Website name:

URL:

Description:

Website name:

URL:

Description:

Website name:

URL:

Description:

Evaluation

Conclusion

London visit webquest (Chapter 2)

Introduction

You and some friends have decided to travel to London for the day on Saturday. Your train arrives at Victoria Station at 10:20, and your train home leaves at 17:35. You have just over seven hours in one of the world's most interesting cities.

Task

You are going to plan your day out in London. You want to see at least three of the most famous landmarks, eg Buckingham Palace; visit one big museum; and do some shopping. Remember, you can walk around the centre of London, but if you want to visit things outside the centre, you need to take the Underground. Your plan should include how much money you will need. Most national museums are free; other tourist attractions charge for entry.

Process

Use the resources to plan your time in London. You do not need to have an exact timetable. Do not forget you need time to get from one place to another, whether you walk or use the Underground. You are taking a packed lunch, so you do not need to research restaurants, but you need to decide on a good place to sit and eat your sandwiches.

Be ready to explain your plan to the rest of the group.

Resources

Map of London

http://maps.google.co.uk/maps
http://www.panoramicearth.com/index.php?europe/england/london
Enter 'London' in the Google Maps search box, then use the controls to zoom in closer and move around the map. To find a good place to sit and eat your lunch, use the Panoramic Earth website.

London Underground

http://www.visitlondon.com/tubeguru
If you decide to travel by Underground, use this website to plan your journey and to find out what is close to each station.

Tourist information

http://www.visitlondon.com
Find the *Essential Guide to London* and click on *Attractions* to find out about places to visit or *Shopping* to find out where to buy things.

Evaluation

You need to have a well-organized day. Do not try to include too much in your seven hours. Think carefully about how to explain your day and why you want to visit the places on your plan. When you are presenting your plan, do not forget that your visit is in the future.

Conclusion

You now know more about what to do in London. You have also practised talking about future plans.

American accents (Chapter 2)

You are going to find a recording of an interview on the Web, listen to it, then report back to the other members of your group.

1 With the group, brainstorm your favourite American movie and pop stars. Choose one name from the list.

Name:_____

2 Now go to the Altavista audio search engine: http://www.altavista.com/audio. Enter *interview* and the name of the person you chose.

3 From the results select an interview that you think is going to be interesting.

4 Listen to the interview and answer these questions:
   · Who is the interviewer?
   · When did the interview take place?
   · Why is the person being interviewed?
   · What is their latest film/CD?
   · Do they tell any funny stories? Summarize one.
   · Have you learned anything new or surprising about the person? What?

   Stop the recording or go back and listen again if you need to.

Make notes here:

5 Prepare to make a short presentation about the interview. Use your notes. Start your presentation:

   I listened to an interview with _____ . He/She was being interviewed by ____
   _____ in _____ .

6 Tell the group about the person's latest film or CD and any funny stories he/she told. Explain any new or surprising information you learned from the interview.

Collocation finder (Chapter 2)

Keyword: _____

Place your word in the centre of the diagram below and brainstorm as many words as you can that collocate with it. Add them to the diagram.

Verbs	Nouns

Adjectives	Phrases

Now search for the word using a search engine. Read through all the collocations you find in the first 30 results. Add any important and useful new items of vocabulary to the diagram above.

Podcast evaluation worksheet (Chapters 2 and 9)

You are going to listen to a podcast to decide whether to recommend it to the other people in your group.

Title of the podcast: _____

URL or RSS feed: _____

Download and listen to an episode of the podcast and answer these questions:

1 What is the theme of the podcast?

2 What subject(s) are discussed in the episode you chose?

3 Did you find the podcast interesting? Give details.

4 How many people spoke in the podcast? How difficult or easy did you find it to understand them? Give details.

5 Was the sound quality of the recording good? Did this affect how well you understood the speaker(s)?

6 Did you learn any new vocabulary from the podcast? Give details.

Use your answers to prepare a short presentation. Do not forget to answer the main question: Do you recommend this podcast to the other members of your group?

Podcast lesson preparation sheet (Chapter 2)

Clip (short summary)

_____

Counter start time

_____

Counter finish time

_____

Vocabulary to pre-teach

_____

URL of transcript or accompanying article

_____

Questions (with counter times if necessary)

_____

Evaluation sheet for use with web-based material (Chapter 3)

Material _____

Aim   *Does the material have a clear teaching aim?*

Design   *Is the material easy to navigate?*

Pedagogy   *Is the material pedagogically sound?*

Interest   *Is the material likely to be of interest to my learners?*

Use   *Is the material usable as it is, or does it need adapting?*

Conclusion   *How would I evaluate the material overall, and would I recommend this material to another teacher?*

Technical considerations _____

Exploring word frequency (Chapter 4)

The *Macmillan English Dictionary* uses colour and a three-star system to show word frequency:

*** (red text)	**the most frequent 2,500 words in English**
** (red text)	**the next most frequent 2,500 words**
* (red text)	**the next most frequent 2,500 words**
No star (black text)	**less frequent words**

1 Which star rating do you think the following words have?

cast (n)   _____

cancer   _____

exposure   _____

hassle (v)   _____

mint (n)   _____

2 Compare your answers with a partner.

3 Check your answer in the *Macmillan English Dictionary* (book or CD-ROM).

Using dictionaries (Chapter 4)

Bilingual paperback/electronic dictionary _____

Advantages	Disadvantages

Monolingual English learner's dictionary _____

Advantages	Disadvantages

CD-ROM _____

Advantages	Disadvantages

Online dictionary _____

Advantages	Disadvantages

Mapping words (Chapter 4)

Create a 'word map'. First, write your keyword in the circle in the centre. Then, add more words in circles which show the different forms of your keyword (eg adjective, adverb etc). Continue to add to your map by including some of the additional information at the bottom of the worksheet.

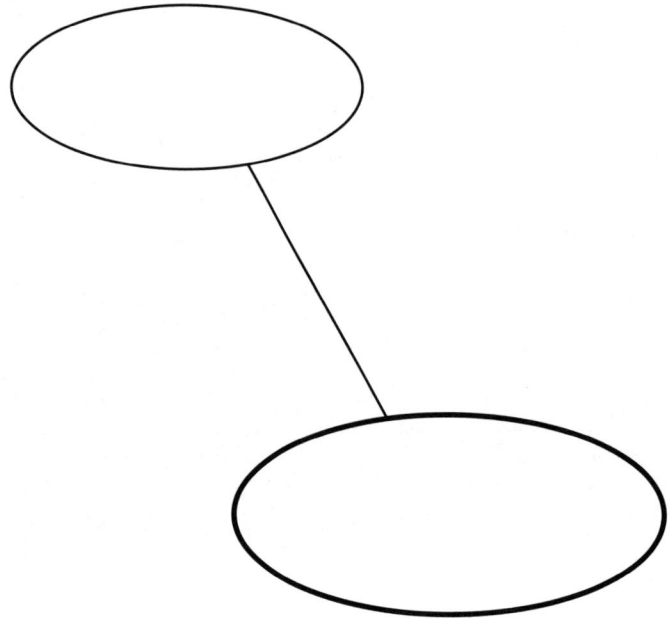

- your own example sentences
- pronunciation notes / word stress
- synonyms / antonyms / related words

- meaning
- collocations
- derivatives

- other forms
- phrases/idioms
- connotation (+/−)

 Blended Learning © Macmillan Publishers Limited 2007. This page may be photocopied and used within the class.

Portable electronic dictionaries (Chapter 4)

Features

Benefits

Drawbacks/Concerns

Email template (Chapter 8)

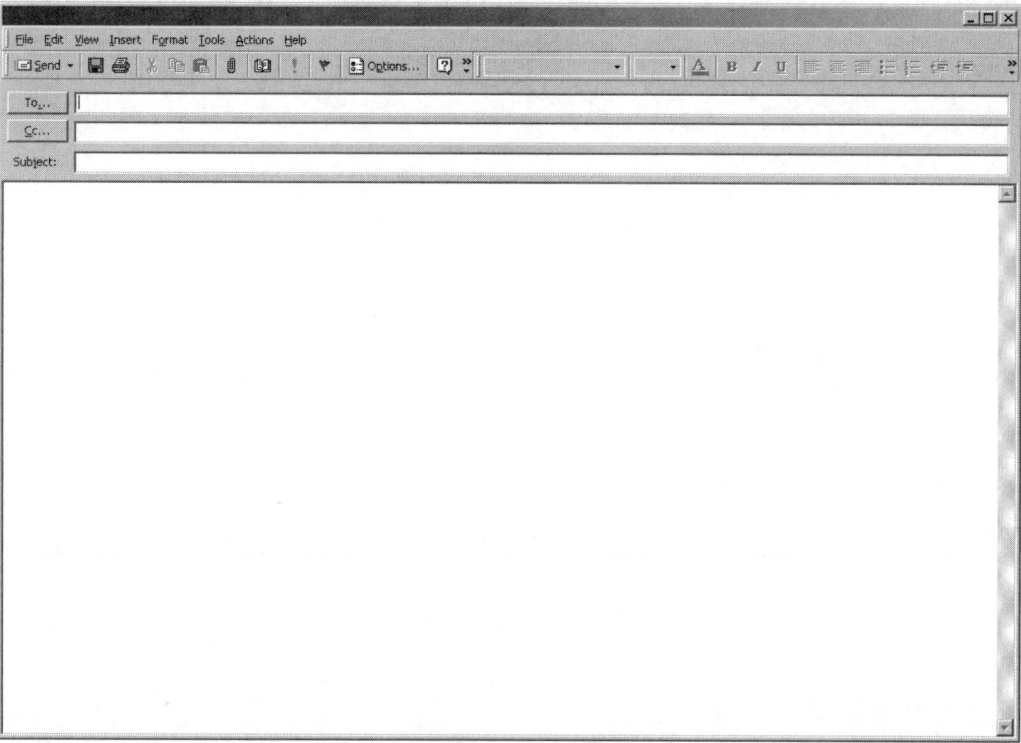

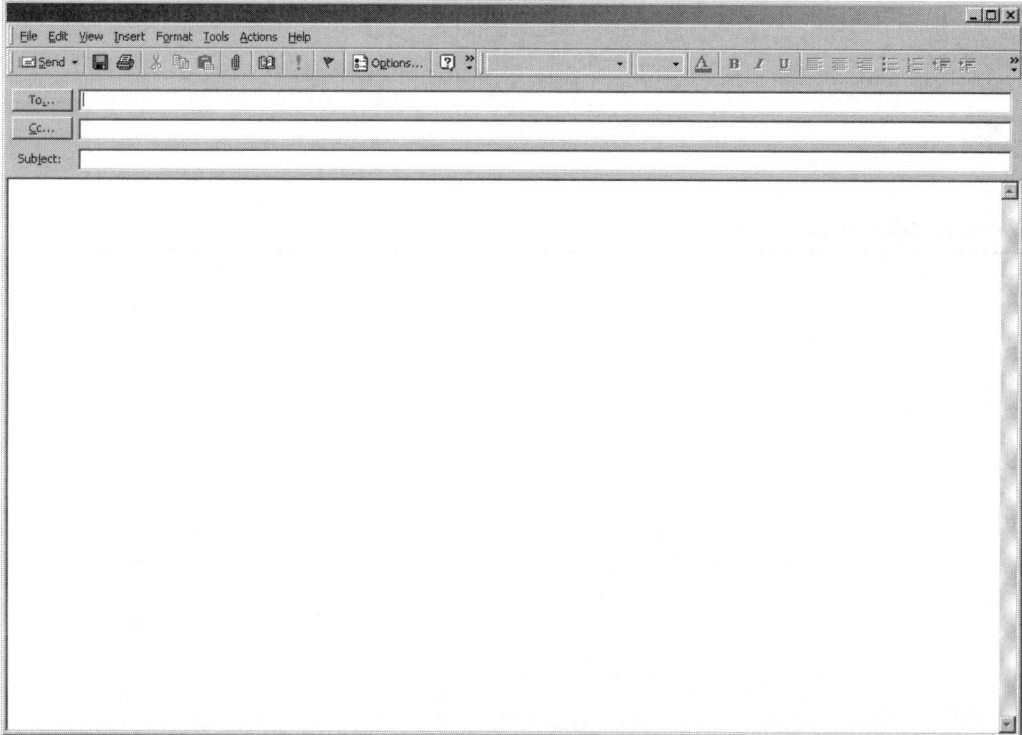

A weekend with a friend from out-of-town (Chapter 8)

A friend is coming to spend the weekend in your home town. He would like you to show him around, as he has never visited your town before. You only have one full day to do so, Sunday.

Chat online to your group and together decide on a plan for the day. Take into account what everyone has to say and write down a plan that you all agree on.

Remember to use only English.

Sunday morning: _____

_____

_____

_____

_____

Lunch: _____

_____

_____

_____

Sunday afternoon: _____

_____

_____

_____

_____

Dinner: _____

_____

_____

_____

Sunday evening: _____

_____

_____

_____

Talky-writing (Chapter 8)

1 What are the differences between speaking and writing?

Writing

mistakes NOT tolerated

Speaking

mistakes tolerated

2 What are the features of emails?

Emails

use emoticons

Blog project planning sheet (Chapter 9)

You are going to set up a blog using Blogger. Before you start, you need to make some decisions and do some preparation.

Stage 1: Subject of our blog

We are going to write about:

☐ our English classes

☐ our hobbies and interests

☐ what's happening in our school/town

☐ what's happening in the news

Stage 2: Setting up the blog using Blogger

Before you start, decide:

- a username and password
- a URL, ie http://*thenameyouchooseforyourblog*.blogspot.com
- a title and, if you like, a subtitle for your blog, which will appear at the top of the web page

Stage 3: Use of the blog

How often are you going to update the blog?

☐ daily

☐ weekly

☐ after each lesson

☐ as and when we have something we want to write

Stage 4: Rules

You need to set any rules about what you can and cannot write in your blog.

Rules for blog writers:

Stage 5: Comments

Are you going to allow people to add comments? Who is going to monitor the comments and delete ones that do not follow the rules for your blog?

Rules for comments added to the blog:

Podcast project planning sheet (Chapter 9)

You are going to record a podcast which you can distribute to other people in your class. Here some things to consider and decide before you start to record your podcast.

Title of the podcast: _____

Length of the podcast: _____ minutes

Content of the podcast

We are going to talk about:

☐ our English classes   ☐ what's happening in our school/town

☐ our hobbies and interests   ☐ what's happening in the news

Format of the podcast

Our podcast going to be:

☐ a monologue   ☐ a conversation (two or more voices)

☐ improvised   ☐ a combination of scripted and improvised

☐ scripted

Names of the speakers

_____   _____

Other considerations

Our podcast needs:

☐ music   ☐ sound effects

Delivery

How are you going to distribute the podcast?

☐ via the school network   ☐ by email

☐ through a website   ☐ with an RSS feed

Rules

You need to set any rules about what you can and cannot say in your podcast.

Photocopiable   *Blended Learning* © Macmillan Publishers Limited 2007.
This page may be photocopied and used within the class.

To gain access to the Web, you require a computer connected to the Internet. This is usually done with an additional electronic device which is connected to a telephone line, to the cable your TV signal comes from or to a large network of computers in a company or on a university campus, for example. This allows you to 'go online', ie connect to the Internet. If you are a novice, then is it advisable to begin by using the equipment and facilities of a friend or of your school or institution before buying your own computer.

Browsers

If you are using a computer running Microsoft Windows, then you probably use Microsoft's browser software, Internet Explorer (IE). Since it is pre-installed on all new Windows computers, IE is the most commonly used browser in the world. If you are using an Apple Macintosh with OSX, you will probably have Safari, Apple's own browser.

There are other browsers available, and the choice of a browser is fairly personal. If you prefer to try something different from IE or Safari, there are other programs which can be downloaded and installed on your computer for free and set to operate as the computer's default browser, ie the browser that is automatically opened when the user accesses the Web. Some of the more popular ones are:

- Mozilla Firefox
  http://www.mozilla.org/products/firefox
- Opera
  http://www.opera.com
- Netscape
  http://browser.netscape.com/ns8

See below for how to download and install programs from the Web.

Viruses

Once a computer is connected to the Internet, it is vulnerable to programs called *viruses* which can damage it. There are other small programs called *spyware*, which can steal information such as passwords and relay them back down the Internet. All these things are done maliciously and indiscriminately. It is important to protect your computer from these things. The only way to do this is to install, keep up to date and use special software.

There are three types of protection:

- **Antivirus software** checks for viruses that might be brought in by email or through insecurities in browsers. If any viruses are found, the software neutralizes or removes them. It is important to keep antivirus software up to date, as new viruses are introduced daily.
- A **firewall** monitors information coming in and out of your computer from the Internet. It looks for and blocks any malicious information, software or direct attacks. Many devices available to connect computers to the Internet have built-in firewalls. If you lack this, you should install firewall software.
- **Anti-spyware software** scans your computer for malicious little programs that can be downloaded and installed onto the computer without your permission. There are many

products available to help protect against this type of program. As with antivirus software, it is important to keep anti-spyware software up to date.

Visit http://www.download.com to find which programs are the most popular and to download and install those which you need.

Connections

The best type of connection is the fastest available to you. However, faster connections are more expensive, and their availability is dependent on where you live and the services being offered there. There are three ways of connecting to the Internet and hence the Web.

Modem

A simple modem will either be built into your computer or may take the form of a separate box which connects your computer and the telephone line. It can be identified by the screeching noise it makes when activated. The fastest speed that such a modem can achieve is around 50,000 bytes a second. Unfortunately, in computer terms, this is not very fast. It is good enough to open web pages which are mostly text and can handle audio such as streamed radio. However, downloading pictures and some of the program installation files mentioned above is a very time-consuming exercise at this speed. Web video is almost out of the question.

Broadband

Once an Internet connection is about ten times faster than 50,000 bytes per second, it can be regarded as broadband. In some places, connection speeds of many megabytes are available. This means that ordinary web pages seem to appear instantly; web video is possible, and program files download in seconds rather than minutes. The cost of this kind of service reflects the increase in speed. Prices, however, are falling.

Network

If the computer you are using is part of the network of a company or institution, then your Internet connection is via this network connection. You will receive broadband speeds. The only drawback may be tighter controls on the type of files you can download and use as a result of strict firewall policies.

How to download and install software

This is a general procedure for downloading software from the Web and installing it on a computer running Windows software.

1 Most websites which offer software for download will direct you to a web page with a button labelled Download. Click on this to start the process.

2 When your computer sees that you want to download a file from the Web, it will ask you whether you want to run the file or to save it. With software installation files, you should select Save.

3 Your computer will then give you the option to decide where you want to save the file. Make sure you save the file somewhere on your computer's hard drive where you will be able to find it again if necessary. Some people make a new folder inside the My Documents folder; others temporarily save it onto the computer desktop. Make your selection and click on Save to start the download.

4 The computer will show you the progress of the download. How long this takes depends on the size of the file and the speed of your connection.

5 Once the download is complete, locate the file and double-click to start the installation process.

6 The installation process of computer software is standardized. You will need to follow the instructions the first few times you do it. However, the more you install software, the more you will become familiar with the procedure and you will thus be able to deal with any variations.

How to uninstall software

You may have installed a program which you do not need, which does not work or which seems to cause problems. If this is the case, then you should uninstall that program. This is the procedure to achieve this on a Windows computer.

1 If the program you want to uninstall is running, close it.

2 Click on the Start button at the bottom of the screen and select Control Panel from the menu.

3 Once the Control Panel window has opened, double-click *Add or remove programs*.

4 You will be shown a list of all the programs installed on your computer. Click once to select the program you want to uninstall.

5 Click on the Remove button and follow the instructions. After you have uninstalled a program, you may be instructed to restart your computer.

Warning: Only uninstall programs you have personally installed. The list of programs in the *Add or remove programs* panel can include some which are vital to the running of your computer, and these should only be adjusted by an expert.

BIBLIOGRAPHY AND REFERENCES

Baber, E. and Hampel, R. 2003 'Using Internet-based audio-graphic and video-conferencing for language teaching and learning'. In Felix, U. (ed.) *Language Learning Online: Towards Best Practice*. Lisse: Swets & Zeitlinger B.V.

Bax, S. 2003 'CALL – past, present and future' *System* 31,13–28.

Claypole, M. 2003 'Blended Learning: new resources for teaching Business English'. In Pulverness, A. (ed.) *IATEFL Brighton Conference Selections*. Canterbury: IATEFL

Driscoll, Dr M. 'Blended learning: Let's get beyond the hype' Accessed from: http://www.ltinewsline.com/ltimagazine

Frendo, E. 2005 *How to Teach Business English*. Harlow: Longman

Herrington, J. D. 2005 *Podcasting Hacks: Tips and Tools for Blogging Out Loud*. California: O'Reilly Media

Jones, C. 1986 'It's not so much the program, more what you do with it: the importance of methodology in CALL', *System* 14/2, 171–178

Salmon, G. 2002 *E-tivities*. Abingdon: RoutledgeFalmer

Scrivener, J. 2005 *Learning Teaching*. Oxford: Macmillan

Smith, D.G. and Baber, E. 2005 *Teaching English with Information Technology*. London: Modern English Publishing

Thornbury, S. 2001 *Uncovering Grammar*. Oxford: Macmillan Heinemann

Willis, J. A. 1996 *Framework for Task-Based Learning*. Harlow: Longman

INDEX